YORK NOTES

KS2 ENGLISH SATS

CATCH UP GRAMMAR, PUNCTUATION AND SPELLING

REBECCA ADLARD

Pearson

YORK PRESS

The right of Rebecca Adlard to be identified as the Author of this
Work has been asserted by her in accordance with the Copyright,
Designs and Patents Act 1988

YORK PRESS
322 Old Brompton Road, London SW5 9JH

PEARSON EDUCATION LIMITED
Edinburgh Gate, Harlow,
Essex CM20 2JE, United Kingdom
Associated companies, branches and representatives throughout the world

© Librairie du Liban *Publishers* 2018

First published 2018

10 9 8 7 6 5 4 3 2 1

ISBN 978–1–2922–3282–9

Typeset by Carnegie Book Production
Printed in Slovakia

Tuzemka/Shutterstock for page 5 / Olga Milksova/Shutterstock for page 6 top / Sandra van der Steen/Shutterstock for page 6 middle / Ints Vikmanis/
Shutterstock for page 6 bottom / conrado/Shutterstock for page 7 / Victor Brave/Shutterstock for page 7 and elsewhere / gorillaimages/Shutterstock for
page 8 top / Ivonne Wierink/Shutterstock for page 9 top / Nattika/Shutterstock for page 9 bottom / Igor Zakowski/Shutterstock for 10 top / Mr Chuckles/
Shutterstock for page 10 middle / Jagodka/Shutterstock for page 11 top / Andrey Kiselev/Shutterstock for page 11 bottom / Delpixel/Shutterstock for
page 12 / Stepan Kapl/Shutterstock for page 13 top / enterphoto/© iStock for page 13 / Chirtsova Natalia/Shutterstock for page 14 top / Alexey Boldin/
Shutterstock for page 15 top / Razvan Ionut Dragomirescu/Shutterstock for page 16 top / Kakigori Studio/Shutterstock for page16 bottom / pixinoo/
Shutterstock for page 17 top / Fotokostic/Shutterstock for page 18 / Fotokostic/Shutterstock for page 18 bottom / Nata-Lia/Shutterstock for page 19 top /
Fejas/Shutterstock for page 19 / kipargeter/Shutterstock for page 20 top / Elena Elisseeva/Shutterstock for page 21 / Grigorita Ko/Shutterstock for page 22
top / Rosa Jay/Shutterstock for page 22 middle / Jiro/Open Clip Art for page 23 and elsewhere / Angyalosi Beata/Shutterstock for page 23 bottom / Golbay/
Shutterstock for page 24 top / naveh/Shutterstock for page 25 / Baibaz/Shutterstock for page 26 / Albina Glisic/Shutterstock for page 26 / Matimix/
Shutterstock for page 27 top / Iaroslav Neliubov/Shutterstock for page 28 / Dotted Yeti/Shutterstock for page 29 top / Marques/Shutterstock for page 29
bottom / Thorir Aron Stefansson/Shutterstock for page 30 / Photo and Vector/Shutterstock for page 31 top / robuart/Shutterstock for page 31 middle /
Duncan1890/© iStock for page 32 top / wiktord/Shutterstock for page 32 / Lane V. Erickson/Shutterstock for page 33 top / Steve Mann/Shutterstock for
page 33 bottom / LORA MARCHENKO/Shutterstock for page 34 top / Visual Generation/Shutterstock for page 34 middle / AS Food studio/Shutterstock
for page 34 bottom / Scc.comics/Shutterstock for page 36 top / Selin Serhii/Shutterstock for page 36 bottom / Eugenecriss/Shutterstock for page 37 top /
cosmaa/Shutterstock for page 39 / Imgorthand/© iStock for page 40 / Lorelyn Medina/Shutterstock for page 41 / BlueRingMedia/Shutterstock for page 42 /
KOLOTAILO LIDIIA/Shutterstock for page 43 / Homydesign/Shutterstock for page 44 / Kudryashka/Shutterstock for page 45 top / Infoland/Shutterstock for
page 45 middle / Fancy Tapis/Shutterstock for page 45 bottom / synchR/Shutterstock for page 46 top and elsewhere / NASA images/Shutterstock for page
46 / Mejnak/Shutterstock for page 47 middle / Pixelbliss/Shutterstock for page 48 middle / RossHelen/Shutterstock for oage 49 middle / BrendanHunter/©
iStock for page 49 bottom / ffolas/Shutterstock for page 50 top/ Studio Grand Ouest/Shutterstock for page 50 middle / YevO/Shutterstock for page 51
top / Eric Isselee/Shutterstock for page 51 / kikovic/Shutterstock for page 52 top / Andrey Kuzmin/Shutterstock for page 53 top / studiolaut/Shutterstock
for page 53 bottom / Diana Taliun/Shutterstock for page 54 top / Sergey Ryzhov/Shutterstock for page 54 / Zefart/Shutterstock for page 54 bottom /
Elena Elisseeva/Shutterstock for page 55 top / Eric Gevaert/Shutterstock for page 56 bottom / Africa Studio/Shutterstock for page 58 top / PhotocechCZ/
Shutterstock for page 58 middle / Claire McAdams/Shutterstock for page 58 / Yayayoyo/Shutterstock for page 59 top / otsphoto/Shutterstock for page 59
middle / Display Intermaya/Shutterstock for page 60 top / Christos Georghiou/Shutterstock for page 61 top / Kostenyukova Nataliya/Shutterstock for 61 /
DLW-Designs/Shutterstock for page 62 middle / ya_mayka/Shutterstock for page 62 bottom / KittyVector/Shutterstock for page 62 bottom / Macrovector/
Shutterstock for page 62 bottom / Yayayoyo/Shutterstock for page 63 top / Yayayoyo/Shutterstock for page 63 top / Ilterriorm/Shutterstock for page
63 bottom / Constantine Pankin/Shutterstock for page 64 top / Constantine Pankin/Shutterstock for page 64 top / Jeka/Shutterstock for page 66 top /
Golubovy/Shutterstock for page 67 top / Kraska/Shutterstock for page 67 bottom / Max Topchii/Shutterstock for page 68 top / AlexeyZet/Shutterstock for
page 68 bottom / Gino Santa Maria/Shutterstock for page 69 / ivkuzmin/© iStock for page 70 / tkemot/Shutterstock for page 71 / yayayoyo/Shutterstock for
page 71 middle / Blan-k/Shutterstock for page 72 / aetb/© iStock for page 73 / Bildagentur Zoonar GmbH/Shutterstock for page 74 bottom / Jeff Feverston/
Shutterstock for page 75 bottom / anela.k/Shutterstock for page 76 top / 32/Shutterstock for page 76 bottom / CKP1001/Shutterstock for page 77 /

CONTENTS

Check Out Grammar!

Check Out Sentences!

Check Out Tenses!

Check Out Punctuation!

Check Out Spelling and Vocabulary!

Answers and Glossary

CHECK OUT GRAMMAR!
NOUNS 1

1 A **noun** **is a word for a** **person, thing or place.**

The boy took a selfie in front of the castle.

NOW YOU TRY!

Underline the nouns in this sentence.

The boy giggled when a seagull photobombed his photo.

TOP TIP ⭐

Remember! Proper nouns start with a **capital letter**.

2 **Nouns for the names of things like** people, places, countries, books, films, historical events, organisations, days and months **are called** proper nouns.

Enid Blyton based Kirrin Castle in her Famous Five books on Corfe Castle in Dorset, England.

The castle was important in the English Civil War and is now owned by the National Trust. We went there one Tuesday in May.

NOW YOU TRY!

Underline the proper nouns in this sentence.

In March, Anna went on holiday to Australia.

TOP TIP ⭐

Look out for the <u>underlined</u> words in this book! They are all examples of the type of word (or **word class**) being explained.

3 **Nouns that are used for things like** feelings **are called** abstract nouns.

The boy showed his anger by throwing a stone at the seagull.

PRACTISE AGAIN!

Underline the abstract nouns in this sentence.

To Mum's amazement, Maya felt sympathy for the seagull and threw it a biscuit.

NOUNS 2

❶ Some nouns **are made up of** two shorter words put together. **These nouns are called** compound nouns.

Toothpaste is a compound noun, made up of *tooth* and *paste*.

NOW YOU TRY!

Draw a line between the two shorter words in each of these compound nouns. The first one has been done for you.

tooth/paste   bedroom   haircut   whiteboard

TOP TIP ⭐

Some compound nouns are two words, e.g. *mobile phone, hot chocolate.*

❷ Nouns used for a group of things, **such as people, animals or objects, are called** collective nouns.

My <u>family</u> ate together: there was Nana Jean, Grandpa Silas, my mum and dad, my two older sisters and me.

NOW YOU TRY!

Underline the collective noun in each sentence.

Selma is playing violin in the orchestra.

The audience clapped loudly.

TOP TIP ⭐

Noun phrases are made up of **one or more adjectives** and a **noun**.

❸ You use a noun phrase **to give** more information about a noun.

adjective + adjective + noun

We have to wear a <u>bright blue uniform</u> to school.

PRACTISE AGAIN!

Underline the noun phrase in each sentence.

I love my soft, grey dressing gown.

My dad makes wonderful biscuits.

The old, rusty car went very slowly.

QUICK QUIZ: NOUNS

1 **Tick** the correct column to show what type of noun each word is.

	Abstract nouns	Proper nouns	Collective nouns	Other nouns
blog				
Trinidad				
happiness				
herd				

2 **Draw** lines to match a word from each side to create compound nouns.

home	pot
tea	pool
play	ground
key	board
swimming	work

3 Look at this photo. **Write** two noun phrases about it.

On the left is a ....

....

She is looking at a ....

....

 *Wow, you're making great progress!*

→ NOUNS →

FINISH

7

PRONOUNS 1

1 **You use a pronoun instead of a noun to avoid repeating the noun in the same sentence.**

When Zara picked up the puppy, the puppy started barking at Zara. ✗

When Zara picked up the puppy, it started barking at her. ✓

NOW YOU TRY!

Underline the pronouns in these sentences.

Marsha is in a play and she won't stop talking about it!

We're going to see it tomorrow night.

2 **Did you see? You use the personal pronoun she, he, you, etc. for a person. You use the pronoun it for things, e.g. *We're going to see it* (it = the play).**

PRACTISE AGAIN!

Complete the sentences with the most suitable pronoun from the box.

> her   they   it   she

Kai wanted to climb the tree, but .... was too slippy.

Marta was so glad to see Rosie, ... hugged ....

Do teachers ever go home? No, ... work all day and all night!

TOP TIP

Some pronouns act as the **subject** of the sentence: *She hugged Rosie.*

Some pronouns act as the **object** of the sentence: *Marta hugged her.*

FIND OUT MORE!

To find out about **subjects** and **objects** in sentences, go to page 22.

PRONOUNS 2

❶ You use a possessive pronoun **to show** who owns something.

There are lots of shoes, Daisy. Which ones are <u>yours</u>?

NOW YOU TRY!

Complete the table with the correct possessive pronouns from the box. The first one has been done for you.

> *its   ours   his   yours   theirs   ~~mine~~   hers*

Personal pronoun	Possessive pronoun
I	mine
you	
he	
she	
it	
they	
we	

TOP TIP ★

Watch out! **My** is a possessive adjective not a possessive pronoun.

PRACTISE AGAIN!

Underline the possessive pronouns in these sentences.

The bag on the table is mine.

That dog isn't his.

Step away from the biscuits — they're ours.

FIND OUT MORE!

To find out about relative pronouns, go to **Relative clauses** on pages 33 and 34.

DETERMINERS

**❶ Determiners give information about a noun.
The determiners *a*, *an* and *the* are called articles.**

In the pet shop, there was a mouse and an elephant!

NOW YOU TRY!

Underline the articles in this sentence.

The snake was coiled around an enormous branch in a cage.

❷ You can use determiners to say which person or thing you are talking about.

This rabbit is fluffier than that one, and these rats are larger than those ones.

NOW YOU TRY!

Circle the correct options to complete the sentence.

If you have a small room, then this / these pet is a better choice than that / those one.

❸ You can use determiners to say how much or how many things there are, or whether there is enough.

There aren't many pets left.

You've had enough time in the shop now.

TOP TIP ⭐

Remember, you use **a** before a word that starts with a **consonant**, and **an** before a word that starts with a **vowel**.

TOP TIP ⭐

Determiners can be **singular** or **plural** to match the **noun** e.g.

This tarantula is cute. (one tarantula)

These tarantulas are terrifying. (more than one tarantula)

PRACTISE AGAIN!

Circle the correct determiners to complete the joke.

Q: There were ten cats in a boat and any / some jumped out.

How many / enough were left?

A: None / More of them — because they were copycats!

❶ Circle all the pronouns in this sentence.

If you see a black cat, please text me because she is ours.

❷ What type of pronoun is in each of the following?
Write PE for a **personal pronoun**, and
write PO for a **possessive pronoun**.

Where did Iris see <u>them</u>? ....

Give Kieran <u>his</u> book back, please. ....

Where's Sam? <u>He</u> is late. ....

Is this scarf <u>yours</u>? ....

❸ Draw a line to match each sentence to the correct determiner and write it in the gap. Use each determiner only once. The first one has been done for you.

In the bakery, there were ....some........ iced buns.   the

Omar didn't want any of .... iced buns, though.   an

He wanted .... doughnut.   some

There weren't .... doughnuts.   a

So Gran bought him .... éclair instead.   any

 *Wow, you're making great progress!*

→ PRONOUNS → DETERMINERS →

VERBS

❶ Verbs are doing or being words.

Mila <u>watched</u> TV while Luke <u>cleaned</u> the kitchen.

Noor <u>lives</u> in India.

NOW YOU TRY!

Underline the verbs in these sentences.

Tara walks to school on Tuesdays, but her mum drives her on the other days.

Ella tidied the mess in her bedroom.

❷ You use verbs in different forms to show when the action or state happens (past, present or future). These forms are called tenses.

Leo <u>was</u> tired.   Leo <u>is</u> tired.   Leo <u>will be</u> tired.

FIND OUT MORE!

For more on **tenses**, go to pages 36–43.

❸ When you ask a question, you use a helping verb.

<u>Do</u> you <u>watch</u> that baking programme?

helping verb + main verb

<u>Can</u> you <u>pass</u> the butter, please?

helping verb + main verb

PRACTISE AGAIN!

Choose the correct helping verb from the box to complete each question.

> Can   Do   Are

.... you going home now?

.... I have a lift?

.... you have enough money for the bus?

ADVERBS 1

❶ Adverbs are words that give information about a verb. They tell you how someone or something (the subject of the sentence) does something.

subject   verb   adverb

The bell rang <u>loudly</u>.

NOW YOU TRY!

Underline the adverbs in these sentences.

The tiger growled menacingly.

Ayla ran upstairs quickly.

The door suddenly opened.

The burglars whispered quietly to each other.

❷ Watch out! Sometimes the adverb goes before the verb, e.g. *The door <u>suddenly</u> opened.* Sometimes the adverb goes after the verb, e.g. *The tiger growled <u>menacingly</u>.*

❸ You also use adverbs to say how sure you are about something. These are called adverbs of probability.

<u>*Maybe*</u> *we could go bowling at the weekend.*

TOP TIP ⭐

Many adverbs are made up of the adjective + *ly*. Remember, change *y* to *i* then add *-ly*, e.g.

*happy →
happily*

PRACTISE AGAIN!

Underline the adverbs of probability in these sentences.

We definitely shouldn't have broken the vase.

Perhaps we could go to the park after school.

I'm certainly not going to get up early tomorrow.

ADVERBS 2

❶ You use some adverbs to say where something happened.

The baby was playing <u>upstairs</u>.

NOW YOU TRY!

Underline the adverbs in these sentences.

You need to wait here.

We spread our toys around.

I had to stand outside.

TOP TIP ⭐

Remember! Adverbs that say **where** something happened go at the end of the **clause**.

❷ You use some adverbs to say when, for how long or how often something happened.

The baby is going for her first swimming lesson <u>tomorrow</u>. (when)

She is <u>still</u> talking! (how long)

She <u>never</u> sees her grandparents. (how often)

❸ Adverbs that say when usually go at the end of the sentence. Adverbs that say how often usually go before the main verb.

PRACTISE AGAIN!

Write the adverbs from the box in the correct columns in the table.

| now   always   later   never   all day   ~~here~~   for a month   nearby |

Where	When	How long	How often
here			

14

1 **Tick** the sentence that uses the word *phone* as a **verb**.

My mum gave me her old phone when she got an upgrade. ☐

I phone my mum to tell her what time I will be home. ☐

2 **Complete** the sentence with an appropriate **adverb**.

If we have time, we could go to the ice-cream café ....

3 **Complete** the table. **Change** each **adjective** into an adverb. Then **write** a sentence using each adverb.

Adjective	Adverb	Sentence
angry		
immediate		
slow		

Wow, you're making great progress!

→ VERBS → ADVERBS →

ADJECTIVES

1 Adjectives **are words that** add more detail about someone or something.

It was a <u>big</u>, <u>scary</u> house.

NOW YOU TRY!

Underline the adjectives in this sentence.

Lucy walked slowly up the long, overgrown path.

2 Did you see? You put adjectives before the noun. You can use more than one adjective to describe the noun, and you sometimes separate them with a comma.

3 You can also put adjectives after the verbs be and feel. If you use more than one adjective after be or feel, you separate them with and.

The wind was cold <u>and</u> strong. Lucy suddenly felt lonely <u>and</u> frightened.

PRACTISE AGAIN!

Add a comma **,** or **write** *and* in the correct places in this passage. The first one has been done for you.

The door opened with a rusty, creaky sigh.

A man stood there. He was very small ugly.

Lucy felt dizzy sick, because she was so scared.

She didn't want to go into the dark cold house, but she knew she had to.

Luckily, that's when the happy smiley pizza delivery man appeared.

COMPARATIVES AND SUPERLATIVES

1 **You use** comparative adjectives **to** compare things.

My snail is <u>faster</u> than yours.

NOW YOU TRY!

Underline the comparative adjective in this sentence.

My worm is longer than Izzy's worm.

2 **With a** short adjective, **e.g.** *fast*, **you make the comparative adjective by adding** *-er*: *faster*. **With a** longer adjective, **you put the word** more **or** less **before it, e.g.** *This bug is less attractive than that one, but more interesting.*

3 **You use** superlative adjectives **to say that something has** the most **or** the least **of a particular quality in a group of things or people.**

My snail is the <u>fastest</u>.

4 **With a** short adjective, **e.g.** *fast*, **you make the superlative adjective by adding** *-est*: *fastest*. **With a** longer adjective, **you put the word** most **or** least **before it, e.g.** *This bug is the least attractive, but the most interesting.*

PRACTISE AGAIN!

Write the comparative and superlative for each of these adjectives.

short .... *intelligent* ....

....

PREPOSITIONS

1 You use a preposition to show a relationship between things or people. You use prepositions to show time, place and cause.

Prepositions of time tell you when something happens or how long it happens for.

The midfielder scored <u>before</u> half time.

Prepositions of place tell you where something or someone is or where they are going.

They ran <u>towards</u> the goal.

Prepositions of cause tell you why something happened. They are made up of two words.

Michaela couldn't play in the second half <u>because of</u> an injury.

NOW YOU TRY!

Underline the prepositions in these sentences.

The goalkeeper jumped into the air.

My team lost because of an unfair red card.

She kicked the ball across the pitch.

2 Prepositions come before nouns. You can also put them before pronouns, e.g. *The ball went straight over her head.*

PRACTISE AGAIN!

Circle the best preposition to complete each sentence.

The ball went <u>because of</u> / <u>over</u> the goal.

I took lots of photos <u>during</u> / <u>because of</u> the game.

My team won <u>thanks to</u> / <u>down to</u> penalties.

1 What sort of **adjective** is each underlined word or pair of words in these sentences? **Write A** for a normal adjective, **write C** for a **comparative** and **write S** for a **superlative**.

You've got the <u>best</u> computer games. ....

This version is <u>more exciting</u> than the previous one. ....

You need <u>quick</u> reactions to play this game. ....

Jess was <u>less interested</u> in the game than Milly. ....

2 **Complete** the table.

Adjective	Comparatives	Superlatives
silly		
	higher not as high as	
tired		
		the most incredible the least incredible

3 **Write** each word from the box on the correct ball.

through
thanks to
because of
on
below
until
around
after

Prepositions of time

Prepositions of place

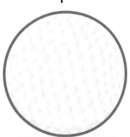

Prepositions of cause

Wow, you're making great progress!

→ ADJECTIVES → COMPARATIVES AND SUPERLATIVES

→ PREPOSITIONS →

CHECK OUT SENTENCES!
STATEMENTS AND QUESTIONS

1 **A** sentence **is a** group of words that make sense together. **Most sentences have a** verb.

I played with the robot.

2 **There are different types of sentences. A** statement **is a sentence that** tells you something.

Jamal made a solar-powered robot.

NOW YOU TRY!

Tick the sentence that is a statement.

I've never made a robot.

Would you like to make a robot?

3 **A** question **is a sentence that** asks something.

Did Jamal make a solar-powered robot?

NOW YOU TRY!

Tick the sentence that is a question.

When did Jamal make the robot?

He had to follow the instructions carefully.

PRACTISE AGAIN!

Add the correct punctuation at the end of each sentence.

Has Jamal ever made a robot before

Jamal brought his robot in to show in our science lesson

TOP TIP ⭐

Remember to read each sentence aloud. Is it telling you something or asking you something?

TOP TIP ⭐

Statements start with a capital letter and have a full stop at the end. Questions start with a capital letter and have a question mark at the end.

COMMANDS AND EXCLAMATIONS

❶ **A** command **is a** sentence **that** tells someone to do something. **Commands contain an** imperative verb. **Imperative verbs are also called bossy verbs, because they can make the sentence sound bossy.**

Before you start cooking, <u>wash</u> your hands.

<u>Wash</u> your hands before you start cooking.

NOW YOU TRY!

Tick the sentence that is a command.

These biscuits are very quick to bake. ☐

Ask an adult to help you put the biscuits in the oven. ☐

❷ **An** exclamation **is a sentence that** shows strong feelings **like anger, shock or excitement. Exclamations start with** how **or** what **and don't always have a** verb.

How yummy these biscuits are!

What a lovely day!

NOW YOU TRY!

Tick the sentence that is an exclamation.

Don't open the oven door yet. ☐

What a lot of mess you've made! ☐

PRACTISE AGAIN!

Add the correct punctuation at the end of each sentence.

What a good cook she is

Offer Nanny a biscuit

How helpful you are

SUBJECT AND OBJECT IN SENTENCES

1 **The subject in a sentence is the person or thing that does the action. The subject often comes before the verb.**

The guinea pig looked sad. Its cage smelled terrible.
Jemma knew it was time to clean it out.

NOW YOU TRY!

Circle the subject in each sentence.

Guinea pigs are rodents. Guinea pigs' teeth never stop growing.

2 **The object in a sentence is the person or thing that the action is done to.**

Jemma picked up the guinea pig. It squealed and bit her.

NOW YOU TRY!

Underline the object in each sentence.

Our class snake, Bob, escaped from his cage.

Bob frightened all the children in the reception class.

He climbed to the top of a very tall tree.

PRACTISE AGAIN!

Circle the subject and **underline** the object in each of these sentences.

A spider ran up Miss Jensen's arm.

Zooey grabbed a glass.

Troy tried to catch the spider.

QUICK QUIZ: SENTENCES

1 What type of sentence is each of the following? **Write S** for a **statement**, **write Q** for a **question**, **write C** for a **command** and **write E** for an **exclamation**.

Poppy, please shut the door. ....

What an annoying laugh that woman has! ....

How long are you staying for? ....

When will you come to my house? ....

My teacher really liked the horror story I wrote. ....

Stop looking at your phone while at the table. ....

2 **Circle** the **subject** and **underline** the **object** in each of these text messages.

I want hot chocolate.

My parents won't let me go to Alice's party.

How does your phone take such great photos?

Mr Townsend cancelled drama club today.

3 **Write** four sentences about this photo:

- A statement: ....
- A question: ....
- An exclamation: ....
- A command: ....

 Wow, you're making great progress!
FINISH

→ DIFFERENT TYPES OF SENTENCES → SUBJECT AND OBJECT →

23

PHRASES AND NOUN PHRASES

1 **This sentence has a subject, a verb and an object.**

subject   verb   object

My mum bought my new trainers online.

A phrase is a group of words without a subject or a verb. You use phrases to give information in a sentence.

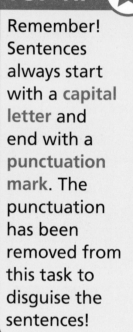

muddy, green trainers

early in the morning

NOW YOU TRY!

Which one of these is a phrase? Tick the correct box.

trainers come in boxes

a pair of brand new trainers

she loves her new red trainers

2 **A noun phrase is a group of words that gives more information about a noun.**

noun

Nimalan has <u>blue trainers</u>.

Nimalan has <u>blue trainers with white stripes on them</u>.

Nimalan has <u>blue trainers with white stripes on them and green laces</u>.

PRACTISE AGAIN!

Underline the noun phrase in each sentence.

I've got a black and white sweatshirt.

There's an enormous sports shop in the centre of town.

Our grumpy PE teacher made us run around the playground.

ADVERBIAL PHRASES

❶ You use an adverbial phrase to give more information about when, where, how or how often something happens.

James woke up with a cold <u>the next morning</u>.

James found a mouldy apple <u>at the bottom of his bag</u>.

James jumped into the river <u>without thinking</u>.

James goes climbing <u>every Monday</u>.

NOW YOU TRY!

Underline the adverbial phrase in each sentence.

I left my new trainers at school.

I get up early every morning to go for a run.

TOP TIP

Read each sentence aloud. Ask yourself which bit gives more information about **when**, **where**, **how** or **how often** the action happened.

❷ You can start some sentences with an adverbial phrase. This is called a fronted adverbial.

<u>Later that day</u>, Year 6 went for a swim in the lake.

PRACTISE AGAIN!

Underline the fronted adverbial in each sentence.

After lunch, we went on the trampolines.

At the end of the walk, we had to go through a river.

In the middle of the forest, there was a trail back to the cabins.

TOP TIP

You put a **comma** after the adverbial phrase when it comes **at the beginning of a sentence**, e.g.

Later that day, Year 6 went for a swim in the lake.

CLAUSES

① A **clause** is a part of a sentence with a subject and a verb.

In these clauses, the subject has been <u>underlined</u> for you and the verb has been (circled.)

<u>We</u> (ate) the fruit salad quickly

because <u>she</u> (smiled) at him

NOW YOU TRY!

Underline the subject and **circle** the verb in these clauses.

My favourite fruit is kiwi fruit.

after I ate all the fruit,

Apples grow in Britain.

when my mum gave me a banana,

The lovely red strawberries tasted delicious.

② **Did you see? A clause can be a complete** simple **sentence that makes sense on its own.**

My favourite fruit is kiwi fruit.

PRACTISE AGAIN!

Tick the clauses.

the ripe, juicy apple ☐

Jai never eats apples. ☐

because he's allergic to apples ☐

QUICK QUIZ: PHRASES AND CLAUSES

1 What type of phrase is <u>underlined</u> in each of the following? **Write N** for a **noun phrase** or **write A** for an **adverbial phrase**.

<u>Last year</u>, my football team won the cup. ....

The ball hit me <u>from above</u>. ....

It was a <u>wet and rainy day</u>. ....

I was covered in mud <u>by the end of the game</u>. ....

<u>After the match</u>, I went to the cinema. ....

2 **Tick** if the sentence has a **fronted adverbial**.

She could see
a boat in the
distance. ☐

Just before bed, I
read a chapter
of my book. ☐

Last night, I
had a crazy
dream. ☐

Trying not to
laugh, George
looked down at
his book. ☐

3 **Write the letter** of each **phrase** or **clause** (a–e) in the correct cloud.

a) *a dishonest little elf with a wand*

b) *He read the book in two days.*

c) *Two days later,*

d) *Dreaming makes me happy.*

e) *In the beginning,*

Noun phrase

Clause

Adverbial phrase

 *Wow, you're making great progress!*

→ NOUN PHRASES → ADVERBIAL PHRASES → CLAUSES →

FINISH

COMPOUND SENTENCES

1 Sentences **can have** more than one clause. **Sentences that have two or more** clauses **that are complete simple sentences are called** compound sentences. **You can join clauses together with words like** and**, or and** but**.**

TOP TIP

Notice how each clause in a compound sentence is a complete **simple** sentence, e.g.

I go to drama club.

I go to art club.

I don't go to karate club.

Clause 1		Clause 2		Clause 3
I go to drama club.				
I go to drama club	*and*	*I go to art club.*		
I go to drama club	*and*	*I go to art club*	*but*	*I don't go to karate club.*

NOW YOU TRY!

Tick the compound sentences.

I'm good at drawing, but I'm not so good at acting. ☐

My swimming class is at 10 o'clock every Saturday. ☐

My mum is learning French and she is learning Spanish. ☐

PRACTISE AGAIN!

Here are some compound sentences about hobbies.

I play cricket on Saturdays and I play football on Sundays.

I don't like dancing, but I do like reading.

Choose verbs from the box and use them to write your own compound sentences about your hobbies.

> *do   like   play   go*

I .... and I ....

I don't .... , but I do ....

CO-ORDINATING CONJUNCTIONS

❶ Words such as and, but and or that join words, clauses or sentences are called co-ordinating conjunctions. When you join two simple sentences together they make a compound sentence.

I like dinosaurs <u>and</u> I enjoy reading about them.

Simple sentence 1	Simple sentence 2	Compound sentence
Some dinosaurs were warm-blooded.	Some warm-blooded dinosaurs ate meat.	Some dinosaurs were warm-blooded **<u>and</u>** they ate meat.
Land dinosaurs were on the Earth a long time ago.	Land dinosaurs became extinct about 65 million years ago.	Land dinosaurs were on the Earth a long time ago, **<u>but</u>** they became extinct about 65 million years ago.

❷ Did you see? To avoid repeating the subject in a compound sentence, you can change the subject to a pronoun, e.g. *dinosaurs ate meat.* → *they ate meat.*

TOP TIP ⭐

If both parts of a compound sentence make sense on their own, you can add a comma before the conjunction: *Sam loves science, but Toby hates it.*

NOW YOU TRY!

Underline the co-ordinating conjunction in each compound sentence.

I don't know anything about where dinosaurs lived or what they ate.

I'm really interested in dinosaurs and I have a lot of books about them.

I used to be frightened of the skeletons in the dinosaur museum, but I'm not any more.

QUICK QUIZ: CLAUSES AND CO-ORDINATING CONJUNCTIONS

1 **Circle** the best **co-ordinating conjunction** to complete each **compound sentence**.

I've got two brothers *and / but* I haven't got a sister.

We went on a school trip to London *but / and* we went to Buckingham Palace.

I fancy fish fingers for tea *or / but* I think we're having pasta.

2 **Make** a compound sentence from each pair of **simple sentences**. Use a suitable co-ordinating conjunction from the links.

My dad likes basketball. He doesn't like football.

....

....

I don't know what I would like for my birthday.
I don't know where to have my party.

....

....

We could go to the park. We could go to the zoo.

....

....

and

or

but

Wow, you're making great progress!

→ CLAUSES IN SENTENCES → CO-ORDINATING CONJUNCTIONS →

FINISH

COMPLEX SENTENCES

❶ **A complex sentence has a main clause (a complete simple sentence) and a subordinate clause, that** only makes sense when you read it with the main clause.

In this complex sentence, the subordinate clause has been underlined for you.

Ava had tomato sauce with her pasta <u>although she doesn't like it.</u>

NOW YOU TRY!

Underline the subordinate clause in each sentence.

Hazel was riding her bike when she saw the squirrel.

Dad was cooking pancakes because it was Pancake Day.

Although it was only 10 o'clock, Maisie and Eva had a midnight feast.

❷ **Did you see? A subordinate clause can come before the main clause**, e.g. *Although it was only 10 o'clock.* **When the subordinate clause comes before the main clause, you put a comma after it:** *Although it was only 10 o'clock, Maisie and Eva had a midnight feast.*

PRACTISE AGAIN!

Find **two** sentences where the subordinate clause comes before the main clause, and insert a comma for each. Remember, a subordinate clause doesn't make sense on its own!

Although she's very old		my nan still has all her own teeth.
Fred was angry with me		because I ate his chocolate.
While Mum was shopping		Nathan cleaned his bedroom.

SUBORDINATING CONJUNCTIONS

1 **You use a** subordinating conjunction **such as** when, if, as, that, once, until, because **and** although **to join a** main clause **to a** subordinating clause.

Henry VIII got very fat <u>as</u> he got older.

He was very fit and active <u>until</u> he injured himself in a tournament.

In his palace, going to the toilet was very sociable, <u>because</u> there were 28 toilets in a row!

TOP TIP ⭐

Watch out! When the subordinating clause is **first** in the sentence, the subordinating conjunction comes at the **start** of the sentence. For example, <u>As</u> Henry VIII got older, he got very fat.

NOW YOU TRY!

Underline the subordinating conjunction in each **complex sentence**.

When Henry VIII's brother Arthur died, Henry married his brother's wife.

Henry VIII beheaded his second wife because he wanted to marry someone else.

Henry changed his mind about wife number four once he had met her.

PRACTISE AGAIN!

Choose the correct subordinating conjunction to complete each sentence.

<u>Although</u> / <u>If</u> Henry VIII was bored with his wife, he found a new one.

Henry VIII had a servant to carry his personal toilet everywhere with him <u>because</u> / <u>until</u> he was the king!

RELATIVE CLAUSES

① **You use a** relative clause **to say** which noun you are talking about.

In these sentences, the **noun** has been (circled) and the relative clause has been <u>underlined</u> for you.

That's the (boy) <u>who broke the window yesterday</u>.

That's the (man) <u>whose zip broke on his coat</u>.

This is the (place) <u>where I found the wallet</u>.

NOW YOU TRY!

Underline the relative clause in each sentence. Then **circle** the noun that each relative clause is describing.

That's the cat which scratched me.

That's the park where I fell off the climbing frame.

② **You use a** relative pronoun **at the** beginning **of a** relative clause.

In these sentences, the relative pronouns have been <u>underlined</u> for you.

That's the boy <u>who</u> broke the window yesterday.

That's the cat <u>which</u> scratched me.

That's the park <u>where</u> I fell off the climbing frame.

That's the man <u>whose</u> zip broke on his coat.

TOP TIP ⭐

You **can** also use the relative pronoun **that** for people, things and animals, e.g.

*the cat **which**/ **that** scratched me* ✓

You **can't** use **what** as a relative pronoun, e.g.

the cat what scratched me ✗

33

Circle the best relative pronoun to complete each sentence.

This the cake <u>that</u> / <u>who</u> I made yesterday.

She's the dinner lady <u>where</u> / <u>who</u> made me eat beetroot.

Can you remember the name of the restaurant <u>which</u> / <u>where</u> we had that lovely pasta?

❸ **Sometimes, the relative clause comes in the middle of the main clause.**

The waiter, <u>who was wearing a blue apron</u>, spilt our drinks.

You use **commas** to show where a relative clause in the middle of a main clause **begins and ends**, e.g.

The squirrel, which was very tame, ate from our hands.

Underline the relative clause in each sentence.

The beans, which were very hot, tasted delicious.

Hannah, who is my best friend, loves macaroni cheese.

Mushrooms, which are my favourite vegetable, are a type of fungus.

Mack, who goes to karate with me, has just become a vegetarian.

QUICK QUIZ: COMPLEX SENTENCES, SUBORDINATING CONJUNCTIONS AND RELATIVE CLAUSES

1 In these **complex sentences**, the **subordinate clauses** have been underlined. **Tick** the one that is a **relative clause**.

I went to Fairlight Primary School <u>until I was 11 years old</u>. ☐

<u>Because my mum is Spanish</u>, I go on holiday to Spain every year. ☐

George loves it when his little brother, <u>who is only three</u>, can't stop laughing. ☐

2 **Add commas** in the correct place or places in these sentences. Watch out: one sentence doesn't need any commas.

That's the person ☐ who runs football club.

Although ☐ I was very hungry ☐ I waited to eat with my friends.

In maths ☐ which is my favourite lesson ☐ we're doing angles.

3 **Complete** each sentence with the correct **relative pronoun** or **subordinating conjunction** from the box.

There's a supermarket on the field .... I used to play.

In the shop I met a woman .... lives on my street.

I want a horse .... I can't ride.

That's Dan, ... daughter is in our class.

.... I leave school, I have to text my dad.

> where
> although
> whose
> when
> who

Wow, you're making great progress!

→ COMPLEX SENTENCES → SUBORDINATING CONJUNCTIONS →

RELATIVE CLAUSES →

FINISH

1 Tense **is the way a** verb **is used to show whether something happens in the** past, present **or** future.

2 You use simple present tense verbs **for what happens now or is a habit.**

Orla <u>is</u> a friendly monster. She <u>lives</u> in a cave and only <u>eats</u> people on Fridays.

NOW YOU TRY!

Underline the simple present tense verbs in this text.

I hunt monsters as a job. Until last year, I worked in a fish and chip shop with my sister, but it bored me. My sister hates her job – she peels potatoes all day.

3 In the simple present tense, regular **verbs have an** -s **added if the subject is** he, she **or** it; e.g. '*I live/she lives*', '*I hate/she hates*'.

PRACTISE AGAIN!

Circle the correct present tense verbs to complete these sentences.

There <u>are</u> / <u>were</u> monsters all over the world. Nowadays, you <u>saw</u> / <u>see</u> them everywhere. My sister <u>found</u> / <u>finds</u> them asleep in her garage all the time. They <u>popped up</u> / <u>pop up</u> in some strange places!

THE PRESENT PROGRESSIVE

❶ You use present progressive verbs to talk about something that is happening now.

I *am reading* a book.

Karen *is watching* TV.

❷ You use different forms of the verb be followed by another verb ending in *-ing*.

NOW YOU TRY!

Complete the table with the present progressive form of each verb. The first one has been done for you.

Simple present	Present progressive			
		Verb *be* (am/are/is)	Second verb + *-ing*	
I read.	I	am	reading	a book.
You ride your bike.	You			your bike.
He feels sick.	He			sick.
We walk to school.	We			to school.
They play football.	They			football.

PRACTISE AGAIN!

Tick the sentences that are in the present progressive tense.

Ali lives in Glasgow. ☐

It is raining. ☐

The children are yawning. ☐

Kim read the whole book yesterday. ☐

THE PRESENT PERFECT

❶ You use present perfect verbs to talk about something that happened or began in the past that has an effect or consequence on now.

Do you want to go swimming?

No thanks, I have been swimming today, so I don't want to go again.

The present perfect can be shown on a time line.

I have been swimming today, so I don't want to go again.

past → present

I went swimming earlier
(past action)

Now I don't want to go swimming again.
(present effect)

NOW YOU TRY!

Underline the present perfect verbs in this sentence.

I know how the story ends because I have watched the film.

❷ Did you see? You use the verb have and a past tense verb to make the present perfect tense.

TOP TIP ★

Imagine a time line for the sentence. Find the past action. This will lead you to the present perfect verbs.

PRACTISE AGAIN!

Write a present perfect sentence using one word or phrase from each cloud.

Subject

I, my teacher, Grandma, this singer, my friends

The verb 'have'

has, hasn't, have, haven't

Past tense verb

been, got, looked, seen, heard, tried

....

QUICK QUIZ: SIMPLE PRESENT, PRESENT PROGRESSIVE AND PRESENT PERFECT

1 Which **tense** is used in each sentence? **Write SP** for the simple present, **write PPR** for the present progressive and **write PPF** for the present perfect.

I am writing a story about ghosts. ....

I have read all the Harry Potter books. ....

Gemma and Emily are playing a game. ....

Priya likes bananas and sugar on toast. ....

My grandad has never played a computer game. ....

2 Which verb form completes each sentence? **Tick** one box for each.

Ben .... to school because he missed the bus.
I hope he gets there on time.

walks ☐

is walking ☐

has walked ☐

What a mess you have made! You .... all your raisins on the floor.

drop ☐

will drop ☐

have dropped ☐

Wow, you're making great progress!

→ SIMPLE PRESENT → PRESENT PROGRESSIVE →

PRESENT PERFECT →

THE SIMPLE PAST

1 **You use the simple past tense for what happened in the past.**

The knight was tired. She climbed onto her horse and returned to the castle.

NOW YOU TRY!

Circle the simple past tense verbs in this text.

Sheila always wanted to be a knight, but her parents said that only boys could be knights. This made Sheila angry, so she took her father's sword and left home. She walked for many miles and for many days, until at last she arrived at the castle of Queen Hanaka, where her dream came true.

2 **Did you see? Some verbs are irregular in the simple past tense: they don't take the -ed ending, e.g. *This made Sheila angry, so she took her father's sword and left home.***

PRACTISE AGAIN!

Circle the verbs that are in the simple past tense.

love	kicked	changed	moved	save	watch
	asked	wanted	decide	shoved	

Change these **simple present tense** verbs into simple past tense verbs.

like ....

discover ....

shout ....

laugh ....

40

THE PAST PROGRESSIVE

1 **You use the** past progressive tense **to talk about something that was happening** at a particular time in the past.

I was sneaking out of the kitchen when Mum turned on the light.

2 **Did you see? You use** was **or** were **followed by another** verb **ending in** *-ing*.

NOW YOU TRY!

Complete the table with the past progressive tense verbs. The first one has been done for you.

Simple past	Past progressive			
		Was or were	Second verb + *-ing*	
I ate the toffee.	I	was	eating	the toffee.
You walked the dog.	You			the dog.
She slept.	She			
We waited for Mum.	We			for Mum.
They practised guitar.	They			guitar.

PRACTISE AGAIN!

Tick the sentences that are in the past progressive tense.

The waves were crashing onto the beach.

The fairground was closed.

Tom is cleaning his teeth.

He was looking on the ground for something.

THE PAST PERFECT

❶ You use the past perfect tense **to talk about something that** happened or began in the past **and has an** effect or consequence on a more recent time in the past**.**

Jamal's hair was wet because he <u>had been</u> swimming.

You can show the past perfect on a time line.

Jamal's hair was wet because he <u>had been</u> swimming.

earlier past   more recent past

Jamal <u>went</u> swimming
(past action)

<u>so</u> his hair <u>was</u> wet
(past consequence)

NOW YOU TRY!

Underline the past perfect tense verbs in this sentence.

When you arrived, I had already left for school.

❷ Did you see? You form the past perfect with had **plus a** past tense verb**.**

TOP TIP ⭐

Imagine a time line for the sentence. Find the past action. This will lead you to the past perfect tense verbs.

PRACTISE AGAIN!

Write a past perfect sentence using one word or phrase from each cloud.

Subject

I, we, the police, the swimmer, my best friend

had

Past tense verb

eaten, thought, found, decided, waited

....

1 Which **tense** is used in each sentence? **Write SP** for the simple past, **write PPR** for the past progressive and **write PPF** for the past perfect.

Dad had tried to make a chocolate cake. ....

Ryan hadn't bothered to do the washing up. ....

Tara and Ayisha were wondering what to do. ....

Selma brushed her hair. ....

The waiter brought our drinks. ....

2 Which verb form completes each sentence?
Tick one box for each.

Dad made a cake for Mum, but the dog .... it before Mum got home.

eats ◻

is eating ◻

had eaten ◻

While Dad .... a nap, Jayden decided to play a computer game.

has ◻

was having ◻

had had ◻

Wow, you're making great progress!

→ SIMPLE PAST → PAST PROGRESSIVE → PAST PERFECT →

MODAL VERBS

 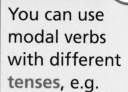
1 **You use** modal verbs **in front of other verbs to talk about** what is likely, possible, necessary or certain.

You can use modal verbs with different tenses, e.g.

You <u>must</u> be home after six o'clock.

They <u>may</u> go swimming after school.

I <u>might</u> be late home after football.

She <u>has</u> to finish her maths homework tonight.

We <u>could</u> be home late tonight.

She **may see** the film. (present simple)

She **may have seen** the film. (past perfect)

NOW YOU TRY!

Underline the modal verbs in these sentences.

They may have gone to Saeed's house.

The film can't have started already.

2 **Did you see? You usually** contract the negative forms **of modal verbs, e.g.**

The film can't have started already.

3 **You can use modal verbs to show** how certain something is.

Sentence B is more likely than sentence A.

A I <u>might</u> learn to play the violin.

B I <u>will</u> learn to play the violin.

PRACTISE AGAIN!

Tick the most certain sentence.

I have to go to town later today.

I may go to town later today.

QUICK QUIZ: MODAL VERBS

1 **Tick** the sentences that contain a **modal verb**.

The girl had forgotten her coat – she must have been cold. ⬭

I might be visiting my cousins at the weekend. ⬭

You may get into the swimming squad this year. ⬭

She had given him her favourite book. ⬭

I had to help my mum wash the car. ⬭

We could have ice cream for pudding. ⬭

2 **Complete** each gap with the best modal verb from the bags.

might   *can*   *must*   *will*

I'm not sure where Kayla is. She .... have gone to the shop.

My singing teacher is going away, so choir practice .... stop over half term.

You .... still join the team, as we need one more player.

3 Look at this picture. **Tick** the sentence that uses the best modal verb to describe it.

He might have fallen off a ladder. ⬭

He can't have fallen off a ladder. ⬭

He has to fall off a ladder. ⬭

45

CHECK OUT PUNCTUATION!
CAPITAL LETTERS AND FULL STOPS

❶ You put a capital letter at the beginning of a sentence and a full stop at the end.

The stars shine at night.

NOW YOU TRY!

Tick the sentence that uses a capital letter and full stop correctly.

Stars produce heat and light ☐

New stars are called protostars. ☐

the hottest stars are blue or white. ☐

❷ You also use capital letters for proper nouns and the pronoun I.

<u>O</u>n <u>S</u>unday, <u>M</u>att and <u>I</u> looked at the night sky from <u>E</u>arth and could see hundreds of stars, but we couldn't see the nearest star, which is the <u>S</u>un.

PRACTISE AGAIN!

Circle the words that should start with a capital letter.

galileo was from italy.

he was born in the town of pisa in 1564.

galileo made the first proper telescope.

in january 1610, he was the first person to see that jupiter has four moons.

he also observed the planets venus, saturn and neptune.

QUESTION MARKS AND EXCLAMATION MARKS

❶ You use a capital letter **at the beginning of a** question, **and a** question mark **at the end.**

What time is it?

NOW YOU TRY!

Tick the sentence that uses a capital letter and question mark correctly.

It's time to go home? ☐

Is it time to go home? ☐

What a lot of time we've wasted? ☐

❷ You use a capital letter **at the beginning of an** exclamation, **and an** exclamation mark **at the end.**

How quickly the afternoon has gone!

PRACTISE AGAIN!

Tick the sentence that uses a capital letter and an exclamation mark correctly.

What a lovely time you've had! ☐

Have you had a lovely time! ☐

Was it a lovely time! ☐

47

QUICK QUIZ: CAPITAL LETTERS, FULL STOPS, QUESTION MARKS AND EXCLAMATION MARKS

1 **Add** the correct punctuation to the end of these sentences.

Where is the party ....

It's in the church hall ....

What fun you'll have ....

Don't forget to take the present ....

2 **Tick** the sentence that uses capital letters correctly.

Mrs ainsley gave me a big chocolate egg for Easter last March. ☐

Mrs Ainsley gave me a big Chocolate Egg for Easter last March. ☐

Mrs Ainsley gave me a big chocolate egg for Easter last March. ☐

3 **Write** a sentence giving your name, your age, the town where you live and the name of your school. Use capital letters and full stops.

....

....

....

....

Wow, you're making great progress!

→ CAPITAL LETTERS → FULL STOPS →

QUESTION MARKS → EXCLAMATION MARKS →

COMMAS

1 **You use** commas **to separate items in a list, and to make a pause in a sentence.**

Dev ate two apples, three bananas, a pineapple, an orange and a bunch of grapes.

NOW YOU TRY!

Insert the missing commas in this sentence.

In my salad, I don't want any lettuce olives carrot tuna red pepper or cheese.

2 **You also use commas to make your meaning clear.**

In the first sentence below, the comma is missing. This changes the meaning.

Zara likes cooking her family and her cat.

Zara likes cooking, her family and her cat.

NOW YOU TRY!

Insert the missing comma in each sentence.

I love my parents Superman and Wonderwoman.

No cycling horses or dogs allowed in the park.

Most of the time travellers need a passport.

Today we're going to cut out and glue kids.

❸ **Don't forget the other uses of commas covered earlier.**

- **A comma after a** fronted adverbial **(see Adverbial phrases on page 25):**

  After dinner, I'm going to watch a film.

- **A comma after a** subordinate clause **in a** complex sentence **(when it comes before the** main clause**) (see Complex sentences on page 31):**

  Even though he wouldn't eat all his pasta, Harry cried when there was no pudding.

- **Commas around** relative clauses **(see Relative clauses on pages 33 and 34):**

  The pie, which was burnt, was too hot to touch.

FIND OUT MORE!

Did you know you can sometimes use dashes or brackets instead of commas? See page 51.

PRACTISE AGAIN!

Insert the missing commas in these sentences.

At the weekend we're going to a pizza restaurant.

Pizza which comes from Italy is very popular in the UK.

Before Niall tasted it he could smell that the fish was not fresh.

BRACKETS AND DASHES

❶ Just like commas around relative clauses, you can use brackets and dashes to show extra information in a sentence.

The dessert (a huge apple pie) smelled delicious.

The dessert — a huge apple pie — smelled delicious.

❷ If the extra information comes at the end of the sentence, you still use two brackets but only one dash.

Amy didn't want to eat the pie (she wasn't hungry).

Amy didn't want to eat the pie — she wasn't hungry.

TOP TIP ★

The correct grammatical term for extra information in a sentence is **parenthesis**.

NOW YOU TRY!

Insert the missing dashes in these sentences.

Snails which are a type of mollusc are eaten in France and Spain.

I'm never going to eat snails that would be disgusting.

PRACTISE AGAIN!

Insert the missing brackets in these sentences.

In China where pandas come from people speak many different languages.

I've never used chopsticks I don't own any.

My dad who travels a lot for work went to China last year.

In Beijing which used to be called Peking he saw the Chinese State Circus.

INVERTED COMMAS/SPEECH MARKS

1 **You use** inverted commas **to** show what someone says.

'I love your new bag,' said Flo.

Gita replied, 'I got it in that new shop.'

2 **Did you see? You put inverted commas before and after the words that are said.**

NOW YOU TRY!

Tick the sentence that uses inverted commas correctly.

'Jack said, Hurry up! The shop is closing.' ☐

Jack said, Hurry up! The shop is closing.' ☐

Jack said, 'Hurry up! The shop is closing.' ☐

3 **Whenever you use inverted commas, you need to use other** punctuation **too!**

When the speech comes first, the punctuation goes inside **the inverted commas.**

'I love your new bag,' said Flo.

'Where did you get it from?' asked Alice.

When the speaker comes first, use a comma in front of **the inverted commas.**

Gita replied, 'I got it in that new shop.'

TOP TIP ★

Inverted commas means upside-down commas.

Inverted commas and speech marks do the same job.

PRACTISE AGAIN!

Insert the missing inverted commas in these sentences.

Mum wants to buy me some new shoes, Saffir said.

Jack said, Can I get some new shoes too?

QUICK QUIZ: COMMAS, BRACKETS, DASHES AND INVERTED COMMAS

1 Which **punctuation** is used in each of these sentences? **Write C** for a comma, **write B** for brackets and **write D** for a dash.

I went to see Fred at the weekend – he's got a new kitten.

Fred's kitten (just ten weeks old and very cute) likes chasing a ball of wool.

While I was playing with the kitten, Fred fed his hamster.

....

2 **Tick** the sentence that uses **commas** correctly.

For supper, we had hot chocolate, cheese on toast and sticky toffee pudding. ☐

For supper, we had hot, chocolate cheese on toast and sticky toffee pudding. ☐

For supper, we had hot, chocolate, cheese, on toast and sticky, toffee, pudding. ☐

3 **Write** a sentence showing what Danni says, using correct punctuation.

I really enjoyed swimming today.

Danni said ....

....

COLONS

① **You use a colon in front of a list.**

I love these colours: pink, white and orange.

NOW YOU TRY!

Insert a colon in the correct place in this sentence.

Jade has three pets a horse, a cat and a dog.

② **You can also write a list using a colon and bullet points.**

To make flapjacks you need:
- *butter*
- *oats*
- *sugar*

NOW YOU TRY!

Rewrite this list as a bulleted list. Remember to use a colon.

Children can choose from the following activities rafting, gymnastics or climbing.

....

....

....

....

③ **You also use a colon to show that two clauses are about the same topic. Usually, the second clause explains the first clause.**

I didn't go climbing: the wall was too high.

PRACTISE AGAIN!

Insert a colon in the correct place in this sentence.

I haven't got any pets my brother's allergic to animals.

SEMI-COLONS

1 Like a comma, you can use a semi-colon as a pause in a sentence.

2 You can use a semi-colon instead of a full stop. It can link two sentences that are about the same thing, to make one sentence.

> *Sara wanted to paint their bedroom green; Holly wanted to paint it yellow.*

> *There were dirty paw prints on the duvet; the cat was looking guilty.*

TOP TIP ⭐

Watch out! Only use a semi-colon if the second sentence links back to the first sentence.

NOW YOU TRY!

Insert a semi-colon in each sentence.

> *John opened the drawer it was empty.*

> *Sally's birthday is in November John's is in September.*

3 You can use semi-colons instead of commas in a descriptive list. This is a list where you are describing each of the items as well as listing them.

(With commas) *At the circus we saw a clown, a fire-eater and an acrobat.*

(With semi-colons) *At the circus we saw a clown juggling with swords and daggers; a fire-eater with flashing eyes; and an eighty-year-old acrobat.*

NOW YOU TRY!

Insert semi-colons in the correct places in this sentence.

> *There are lots of things I have to do over half term: visit Grandma and Grandad learn to play the guitar build a castle out of plastic bricks sell old toys at a car boot sale and paint my bedroom walls orange.*

TOP TIP ⭐

A semi colon is needed before the last item in the list (before **and** or **or**).

QUICK QUIZ: COLONS AND SEMI-COLONS

1 **Tick** the sentence that uses the **colon** correctly.

My legs are tired: I ran five kilometres. ☐

I ran five kilometres: Emily only ran three. ☐

2 **Tick** the sentence that uses **semi-colons** correctly.

For my birthday, I got an enormous jungle
building set; a remote-controlled car that can flip
over; a new sweatshirt with stripes on it;
and some great books on how to draw cartoons. ☐

For my birthday, I got a building set; a remote-
controlled car; a sweatshirt; and some books. ☐

3 **Insert** a **comma**, colon or semi-colon in each box.

I can't come out to play ☐ I'm very busy.

There are five people in my family ☐ me ☐ my mum ☐ my dad ☐
my sister and my brother.

At the farm, you can feed the lambs ☐ help to milk the cows ☐
brush the ponies ☐ and collect the eggs.

Wow, you're making great progress!

→ COLONS → SEMI-COLONS →

FINISH

APOSTROPHES 1

1 An **apostrophe** shows missing letters. You can use an apostrophe to make two words into one shorter word by taking away some letters. The apostrophe shows where the missing letter or letters would be.

it is → it's

there is → there's

cannot → can't

I am → I'm

NOW YOU TRY!

Match each pair of words on the left with the correct contracted form on the right. One has been done for you.

do not	we'll
will not	they'd
could have	could've
there is	we'd
she is	there's
we will	won't
we had	she's
they would	don't

PRACTISE AGAIN!

Write out the contractions in **bold** in full with no apostrophes.

I'm so upset. My cousin said she'd take me shopping, but now her car's broken down and she can't come. I'll have to stay at home!

I'm ....

she'd ....

car's ....

can't ....

I'll ....

APOSTROPHES 2

❶ Apostrophes also show who something belongs to.

Kit's watch → The watch belongs to Kit.

the kitten's bowl → The bowl belongs to the kitten.

❷ If the thing belongs to only one person or thing, you add an apostrophe and an -s, e.g.
The cat has a bowl. → It is the cat's bowl.

NOW YOU TRY!

Rewrite this sentence using an apostrophe and an -s. The first words of the sentence have been written for you.

This toy belongs to my dog.

This toy is ....

❸ If the thing belongs to more than one person or thing, you only add the apostrophe.

Zebras' stripes are all different.

PRACTISE AGAIN!

Tick the sentence in which the apostrophe shows that the shoes belong to more than one dancer.

The dancer's shoes.

The dancers' shoes. ⬜

1 **Underline** the pair of words that can be contracted in each sentence. Then **write** the contractions.

The policewoman could not understand how the burglar got away. ....

She did not know that the burglar was still in the building! ....

2 Which type of **apostrophe** is in each of these sentences? **Write C** for contraction and **write P** for possession.

I am Leo's best friend.

....

Leo's my best friend.

....

Gracie's best friend is Lin.

....

3 **Look** at the photo. **Write** a sentence using an apostrophe of possession.

Poppy!

These are ....

CHECK OUT SPELLING AND VOCABULARY!
PLURALS 1

1 Plural **means** more than one of something. To show that there is more than one, you usually add -s to the noun.

singular   plural

one wand → two wands

NOW YOU TRY!

Write the plurals of these words.

spell   wizard   cat   owl   broomstick

....

....

....

2 For some nouns, you have to change the spelling in the plural form.

singular   plural

one child → six children

a woman → two women

PRACTISE AGAIN!

Match the singular and plural forms of these irregular nouns.

man	people
tooth	men
person	mice
mouse	feet
foot	teeth

TOP TIP ⭐

Did you know? **Singular** means one of something. Singular is related to the word single, which means one on its own.

TOP TIP ⭐

Watch out! Some nouns do not have a different plural form. For example:

one fish → three fish → a whole saucepan of fish

Other examples include sheep, moose and deer.

PLURALS 2

1 **Some nouns have different spelling rules for their plural forms. If a noun ends in** *-ch*, *-s*, *-sh*, *-ss* **or** *-x*, **you add** *-es*. **If it ends in** *-z*, **you double the** *z* **and add** *-es*.

*one **wish** → three wish**es***

*a **quiz** → a book of quiz**zes***

2 **For nouns that end in a consonant +** *y*, **you change the** *y* **to an** *i* **and add** *-es*.

*the **story** of Aladdin → many **stories** about Aladdin*

NOW YOU TRY!

Write the plurals of these words.

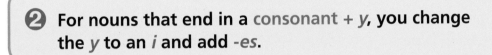

baby   eyelash
dress   box   witch
gas

....

....

3 **For some nouns that end in an** *-o* **you add** *-es*. **These include:** *tomato, hero, echo, domino* **and** *mango*.

Aladdin went to the market and bought a tomato. →
*Aladdin went to the market and bought a bag of tomat**oes**.*

4 **For nouns that end in** *-f* **or** *-fe*, **you change** *f* **or** *fe* **to a** *v* **and add** *-es*.

*The princess wore a blue scar**f**. → The princess wore some blue scar**ves**.*

PRACTISE AGAIN!

Write the plurals of these words.

mango   half
thief   hero

....

....

QUICK QUIZ: PLURALS

REMEMBER THE RULES!

Nouns	Rule	Example
most nouns	add -s	cat → cats
ending -ch, -s, -sh, -ss	add -es	beach → beaches
ending -z	add -zes	quiz → quizzes
ending in consonant + -y	change -y to -i + -es	party → parties
ending -o	add -es	potato → potatoes
ending -f or -fe	change -f or fe to -v + -es	hoof → hooves

Some nouns are irregular.

❶ **Tick** the plurals that are correct.

geese ☐

swans ☐

leafs ☐

pizzas ☐

partys ☐

deers ☐

❷ **Write** what you can see.

 ....

 ....

 ....

 ....

 *Wow, you're making great progress!*

→ PLURALS →

PREFIXES 1

❶ A prefix is a group of letters that you put in front of a word to change its meaning.

I'm happy. → *I'm <u>un</u>happy.*

❷ Watch out! You don't change the spelling of the original word when you add a prefix.

NOW YOU TRY!

Match each word with the correct prefix to change its meaning.

Prefix	Word
un	behave
dis	do
in	appear
mis	correct

PRACTISE AGAIN!

Write each prefix from the box in front of a word below to make five new words.

un	under	super	re	sub

......................market

......................draw

......................expected

......................marine

......................age

PREFIXES 2

① Prefixes have different meanings. For example, you use the prefixes *un-* and *dis-* to give some words their opposite meaning.

My laces are done up. → My laces are **un**done.

NOW YOU TRY!

Read these sentences.

In America, they call the underground the **subway**.

Have you seen the **preview** of the new Marvel film?

I like the bit where you can't see him because he's **invisible**.

Can you **resend** your text, please? It hasn't arrived.

I prefer reading **nonfiction** to fiction.

I didn't get the answer right because I **misunderstood** the question.

Draw lines to match each correct prefix with its meaning.

Prefix:	mis	in	re	non	sub	pre

Meaning:	do again	without or not	wrong or bad	before	not	below or under

TOP TIP ⭐

Remember! You can put a prefix in front of a **noun**, an **adjective** or a **verb**.

FIND OUT MORE! 🔍

To find out about **nouns**, **verbs** and **adjectives**, go to **Check Out Grammar on pages 5–19!**

PRACTISE AGAIN!

Write each word in the correct column of the table to show whether it's a noun, a verb or an adjective. Three words have been written for you.

~~subway~~ preview ~~invisible~~ ~~resend~~ nonfiction misunderstood

Nouns	Verbs	Adjectives
subway	resend	invisible

QUICK QUIZ: PREFIXES

REMEMBER THE RULES!

Prefixes **go** before **the** root word.

The spelling of the root word **doesn't change.**

❶ **Underline** the six words with prefixes in this passage.

My little brother was in a lot of trouble today. My mum's phone magically disappeared this morning. Mum said that she was very disappointed in my brother. This made him very unhappy. He said it was impossible that he had taken it, as he had been in his bedroom all morning. Mum said that was nonsense. Anyway, the phone magically reappeared after lunch.

❷ **Write** a sentence for each of these prefixed words.

a) *disagree*   b) *unlucky*   c) *remind*   d) *subtract*

....

....

....

....

....

....

Wow, you're making great progress!

→ PREFIXES →

FINISH

SUFFIXES 1

❶ A suffix is a group of letters that you put at the end of a word to change its meaning.

Jade likes to paint. → *Jade is paint<u>ing</u>.* → *Yesterday, Jade paint<u>ed</u> a landscape.*

Jade is a wonder<u>ful</u> paint<u>er</u>.

NOW YOU TRY!

Draw a line between each word and its suffix. The first one has been done for you.

> fright|en   walked   honestly
> carefully   amazement   crying

❷ When you add the suffix *-ed* or *-ing* to a verb it changes the tense.

simple present   present progressive   simple past

Jade likes to paint.   *Jade is paint<u>ing</u>.*   *Yesterday, Jade paint<u>ed</u> a landscape.*

PRACTISE AGAIN!

What tense is each of these **verbs** in? **Write SP** for the simple present, **write PP** for the present progressive and **write P** for the simple past.

Yana texts Joe every day.   ....

Yana texted Joe at 11.   ....

Yana is texting Joe now.   ....

FIND OUT MORE!

To find out about **tenses**, go to **Check Out Tenses** on pages 36–43.

SUFFIXES 2

① You sometimes have to change the spelling of a word when you add a suffix.

② **Drop the e rule:** if a short word ends in an -e and the suffix starts with a vowel, drop the e then add the suffix.

dance → dancer

NOW YOU TRY!

Add the suffix to each word to change its meaning.

score + ed .... *skate + ing* ....

③ **Change y to i rule:** if the word ends with a consonant and a *y*, change the *y* to an *i* then add the suffix – but *not* if the suffix is *-ing*.

carry → carried   carry → carrying ✓

NOW YOU TRY!

Add the suffix to each verb to change its meaning.

happy + er .... *party + ing* ....

④ **Double it rule:** if a short verb ends with one vowel and a consonant (but *not* w, x or y), double the consonant then add *-ing* or *-ed*.

PRACTISE AGAIN!

Which spelling is correct in each pair? **Circle** the correct spelling.

chopped / choped   *huming / humming*

SUFFIXES 3

1 **You can add some suffixes to adjectives to make them into nouns.**

adjective   noun

Maddie felt sad. There was a lot of sad<u>ness</u> in the class when the teacher retired.

NOW YOU TRY!

Add the suffix *-ness* to each adjective to make a noun.

sick .... cheerful ....

2 **You can also add some suffixes to verbs to make them into nouns.**

verb   noun

Maddie likes to climb. Her mum is a climb<u>er</u> too.

TOP TIP

If a suffix starts with a **consonant**, you don't usually need to change the spelling of the **root word**.

NOW YOU TRY!

Add the suffix *-er* or *-ment* to each verb to make a noun.

build .... excite ....

dance .... agree ....

3 **You can add the suffixes *-ful* (full of) and *-less* (without) to nouns to make them into adjectives.**

noun   adjective   adjective

I hate pain. An injection should be pain<u>less</u>, but it was really pain<u>ful</u>.

PRACTISE AGAIN!

Write the correct suffixes to complete this sentence.

Superman is a power....................... superhero; however, kryptonite makes him power....................... .

SUFFIXES 4

1 **You can add** suffixes **to some** adjectives **to make** adverbs**.**

adjective   adverb

The frog was quick. It jumped quickly into the water.

NOW YOU TRY!

Choose an adjective from the box and turn it into an adverb using the suffix *-ly*, to complete each sentence.

> usual   loud   bad

Mrs Moffitt called .... to her sister, who was a little deaf.

You don't .... see owls in the day.

*Henry had sewn his cushion ....,
so all the fluff came out of the middle.*

TOP TIP ★

If the adjective ends in consonant + *y*, change *y* to *i* and add *-ly* to make the adverb.
*happy →
happily*

2 **If the adjective ends in** *-le,* **you** drop the e **and add** *-y* **to make the adverb.**

terrible → terribly

3 **If the adjective ends in** *-c,* **add the suffix** *-ally* **to make the adverb.**

adjective   adverb

The play was very dramatic. My sister cried dramatically at the end.

PRACTISE AGAIN!

Add the correct suffix to each adjective to turn it into an adverb.

athletic .... *horrible* .... *scary* ....

historic .... *nice* .... *angry* ....

QUICK QUIZ: SUFFIXES

REMEMBER THE RULES!

Drop the e rule: if the word ends in *-e* and the suffix starts with a vowel, drop the e and add the suffix.

Change y to i rule: if the word ends in a consonant plus *-y*, change y to i and add the suffix (but not for *-ing*).

Verb + *-ed* or *-ing* = change in tense

Double it rule: if the short verb ends in a vowel plus consonant (not *w, x* or *y*), double the consonant and add the suffix.

Adjective + *-ly* = adverb

If the adjective ends in *-le*, to make the adverb drop the e and add *-y*.

If the adjective ends in *-c*, to make the adverb add *-ally*.

1 **Underline** fifteen words with **suffixes**.

Umberto the parrot danced comically around the room. Grandad laughed loudly as Umberto swung on a trapeze. Then the parrot cheekily spat a seed at Grandad. Harriet was looking at Umberto in admiration. 'He's amazing,' she told Grandad. Umberto nodded in agreement. A wave of tiredness suddenly came over the little parrot and he climbed carefully onto Harriet's lap and fell asleep instantly.

2 **Write** a **sentence** for each of the following words.

| luckily | fearless | colourful | disagreement |

....

....

....

....

Wow, you're making great progress!

→ SUFFIXES →

WORD FAMILIES

① **Some words are part of a word family – they have the same short word or letters in them. The short word or group of letters is called the root.**

root

clear, _clearly_, un_clear_

NOW YOU TRY!

Underline the root in each word of this word family.

action, actor, react, activity

② **The root links these words so that they have a similar meaning, even if they refer to different things.**

_ped_estrian, _ped_al, bi_ped_, centi_ped_e (_ped_ means _foot_)

_memor_y, re_mem_ber, _memor_ial (_mem_ or _memor_ means _remember_)

TOP TIP ⭐

Finding the root in a word you don't know can help you work out the meaning. If you know that the root in the word _biped_ is _ped_, which means foot, and that the prefix _bi_ means two, then you may be able to work out that a _biped_ is an animal with two feet – like you!

NOW YOU TRY!

Complete the word family table with the words from the box. The first one has been done for you.

~~photograph~~ kilogram audience kilometre
audition graphics paragraph kilobyte audio

kilo (means 1000)	graph (means write or record)	aud (means hear)
	photograph	

SYNONYMS AND ANTONYMS

❶ Synonyms are words that have the same or a similar meaning. Synonyms make your writing more interesting.

Lisa is really <u>chatty</u>, but Anya is even more <u>talkative</u>.

NOW YOU TRY!

Draw a line to match each word on the left with its synonym on the right.

cold	fearless
brave	speak
old	massive
huge	chilly
talk	ocean
sea	elderly

TOP TIP ⭐

Remember! There are synonyms for **verbs, nouns, adverbs and adjectives.**

❷ Antonyms are words that have the opposite meaning to each other.

Yesterday the sea was really <u>rough</u>, but today it is <u>calm</u>.

PRACTISE AGAIN!

Draw a line to match each word on the left with its antonym on the right.

hungry	boiling
freezing	short
tall	tame
quickly	slowly
wild	ugly
beautiful	full

QUICK QUIZ: WORD FAMILIES, SYNONYMS AND ANTONYMS

REMEMBER THE RULES!

A **root** shows that words belong to the same word family and share a similar meaning.

Synonyms mean the same or something similar, **such as:** hot and boiling.

Antonyms mean the opposite, **such as:** hot and cold.

❶ What does the root <u>cent</u> mean in the word family below?
Tick one box.

> <u>cent</u>imetre   <u>cent</u>ury   per<u>cent</u>

time   ☐

a hundred   ☐

family   ☐

❷ **Replace** each <u>underlined</u> word with a suitable synonym from the box.

*The night was <u>pitch black</u> ...., and the
<u>rider</u> .... was feeling <u>anxious</u> ....*

*He wasn't <u>sure</u> .... his horse knew the way
<u>onwards</u> ....*

> ahead
> horseman
> worried
> certain
> dark

❸ What are the underlined words in these sentences?
Write A for antonyms and **write S** for synonyms.

*The bananas had gone <u>mouldy</u> and the apples
were <u>rotten</u>.*   ....

*The rabbit ran <u>fast</u> but the tortoise
ran <u>slowly</u>.*   ....

 *Wow, you're making great progress!*

→ WORD FAMILIES → SYNONYMS → ANTONYMS →

HOMOPHONES

① **Homophones** are words that sound the same **but have** different spellings **and** different meanings.

They're looking for their gloves, which were there on the chair yesterday.

These three words all sound the same, but:

They're is the contracted form of *they are*.

Their is the possessive pronoun, which shows who something belongs to.

There says where something is.

TOP TIP ⭐

To check whether you've got the correct spelling of 'over th**ere**', ask yourself, 'Is it h**ere**, th**ere** or everywh**ere**?' All these words also end in **-ere**.

NOW YOU TRY!

Read the sentences then **write** each <u>underlined</u> homophone next to its meaning.

I read a <u>tale</u> once about a cow with a magic <u>tail</u>.

- *part of an animal* ....

- *story* ....

I <u>heard</u> a <u>herd</u> of cows mooing.

- *listened to* ....

- *group (of animals)* ....

PRACTISE AGAIN!

Underline the homophones in these sentences.

It makes me groan every time an adult says how much I've grown.

The bubble man blew blue bubbles.

I looked in the mirror and noticed that my eye was red.

SILENT LETTERS AND UNSTRESSED VOWELS

❶ **Some words have letters that are silent – this means you don't hear them when you say the word.**

k<u>n</u>ight   <u>g</u>nome   w<u>h</u>ich   ta<u>l</u>k   tom<u>b</u>

❷ **Here are some silent letters to look out for.**

Silent *g* before *n* <u>g</u>naw	Silent *k* before *n* <u>k</u>nee	Silent *h* after *w* w<u>h</u>en
Silent *w* before *r* <u>w</u>rong	Silent *w* before *h* <u>w</u>hole	Silent *b* after *m* dum<u>b</u>
Silent *h* before *o* <u>h</u>our	Silent *u* after *g* g<u>u</u>ess	Silent *l* ha<u>l</u>f term

NOW YOU TRY!

Say these words and **write** them in the correct places in the table above.

> what   disguise   design   calm   guest
> know   thumb   ghost   wrist   knife   comb

❸ **When you say some words, the vowels *a, e, i* or *o* sound like 'uh'. These are called unstressed vowels, e.g.** *library, cinema, offer, family, doctor.*

PRACTISE AGAIN!

Say these words and then **circle** the unstressed vowels.

> listen   undone   familiar   happily

QUICK QUIZ: HOMOPHONES, SILENT LETTERS AND UNSTRESSED VOWELS

REMEMBER THE RULES!

Homophones sound the same but have different spellings and meanings: *their / they're / there.*

Some words have silent letters: *comb, whole.*

Some words have unstressed vowels: *carrot, thunder, gardening.*

1 **Circle** the correct homophone to complete each sentence.

I had to go to the nurse to get my <u>weight</u> / <u>wait</u> checked.

They couldn't see the boat because of the <u>mist</u> / <u>missed</u> coming off the sea.

You should never <u>waist</u> / <u>waste</u> food.

I think I've had <u>too</u> / <u>to</u> much pudding.

<u>Wood</u> / <u>Would</u> you like to come to my party?

2 Say each of these words aloud. **Write S** if it has a silent letter and **write U** if it has an unstressed vowel.

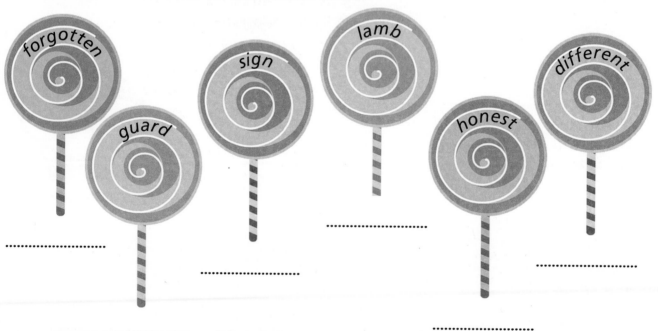

forgotten

guard

sign

lamb

honest

different

 *Wow, you're making great progress!*

→ HOMOPHONES → SILENT LETTERS → UNSTRESSED VOWELS →

76

ANSWERS

CHECK OUT GRAMMAR!

Nouns 1

The <u>boy</u> giggled when a <u>seagull</u> photobombed his <u>photo</u>.

In <u>March</u>, <u>Anna</u> went on holiday to <u>Australia</u>.

To Mum's <u>amazement</u>, Maya felt <u>sympathy</u> for the seagull and threw it a biscuit.

Nouns 2

tooth|paste   bed|room   hair|cut   white|board

Selma is playing violin in the <u>orchestra</u>.

The <u>audience</u> clapped loudly.

I love my <u>soft, grey dressing gown</u>.

My dad makes <u>wonderful biscuits</u>.

The <u>old, rusty car</u> went very slowly.

Quick Quiz: Nouns

1.

	Abstract	Proper	Collective	Other
blog				✓
Trinidad		✓		
happiness	✓			
herd			✓	

2.

homework

teapot

playground

keyboard

swimming pool

3. **Sample answers:**

On the left is a <u>tiny girl</u>.

She is looking at a <u>huge black dog</u>.

Pronouns 1

Marsha is in a play and <u>she</u> won't stop talking about <u>it</u>!

<u>We</u>'re going to see <u>it</u> tomorrow night.

Kai wanted to climb the tree, but <u>it</u> was too slippy.

Marta was so glad to see Rosie, <u>she</u> hugged <u>her</u>.

Do teachers ever go home? No, <u>they</u> work all day and all night!

Pronouns 2

Personal pronoun	Possessive pronoun
I	mine
you	yours
he	his
she	hers
it	its
they	theirs
we	ours

The bag on the table is <u>mine</u>.

That dog isn't <u>his</u>.

Step away from the biscuits – they're <u>ours</u>.

Determiners

<u>The</u> snake was coiled around <u>an</u> enormous branch in <u>a</u> cage.

If you have a small room, then (this) pet is a better choice than (that) one.

Q: There were ten cats in a boat and (some) jumped out.

How (many) were left?

A: (None) of them– because they were copycats.

Quick Quiz: Pronouns and determiners

1. If (you) see a black cat, please text (me) because (she) is (ours.)

2. Where did Iris see <u>them</u>? **PE**

   Give Kieran <u>his</u> book back, please. **PO**

   Where's Sam? <u>He</u> is late. **PE**

   Is this scarf <u>yours</u>? **PO**

3. In the bakery, there were <u>some</u> iced buns.

   Omar didn't want any of <u>the</u> iced buns, though.

   He wanted <u>a</u> doughnut.

   There weren't <u>any</u> doughnuts.

   So Gran bought him <u>an</u> éclair instead.

Verbs

Tara <u>walks</u> to school on Tuesdays, but her mum <u>drives</u> her on the other days.

Ella <u>tidied</u> the mess in her bedroom.

<u>Are</u> you going home now?

<u>Can</u> I have a lift?

<u>Do</u> you have enough money for the bus?

Adverbs 1

The tiger growled <u>menacingly</u>.

Ayla ran upstairs <u>quickly</u>.

The door <u>suddenly</u> opened.

The burglars whispered <u>quietly</u> to each other.

We <u>definitely</u> shouldn't have broken the vase.

<u>Perhaps</u> we could go to the park after school.

I'm <u>certainly</u> not going to get up early tomorrow.

Adverbs 2

You need to wait <u>here</u>.

We spread our toys <u>around</u>.

I had to stand <u>outside</u>.

Where	When	How long	How often
here	now	for a month	always
nearby	later	all day	never

Quick Quiz: Verbs and adverbs

1. I phone my mum to tell her what time I will be home. ✓

2. Sample answer:

If we have time, we could go to the ice cream-café <u>later/tomorrow/soon</u>.

3.

Adjective	Adverb	Sentence
angry	angrily	Sample answer: She threw her bike down angrily.
immediate	immediately	Sample answer: He picked up the phone immediately.
slow	slowly	Sample answer: Her grandad moves very slowly now he's 83.

Adjectives

Lucy walked slowly up the <u>long</u>, <u>overgrown</u> path.

The door opened with a rusty, creaky sigh.

A man stood there. He was very small <u>and</u> ugly.

Lucy felt dizzy <u>and</u> sick, because she was so scared.

She didn't want to go into the dark, cold house, but she knew she had to.

Luckily, that's when the happy, smiley pizza delivery man appeared.

Comparatives and superlatives

My worm is <u>longer</u> than Izzy's worm.

short → shorter → shortest

intelligent → more/less intelligent → most/least intelligent

Prepositions

The goalkeeper jumped <u>into</u> the air.

My team lost <u>because of</u> an unfair red card.

She kicked the ball <u>across</u> the pitch.

The ball went (over) the goal.

I took lots of photos (during) the game.

My team won (thanks to) penalties.

Quick Quiz: Adjectives, comparatives and superlatives, and prepositions

1. You've got the <u>best</u> computer games. **S**

   This version is <u>more exciting</u> than the previous one. **C**

   You need <u>quick</u> reactions to play this game. **A**

   Jess was <u>less interested</u> in the game than Milly. **C**

2.

Adjective	Comparative	Superlative
silly	sillier not as silly as	the silliest the least silly
high	higher not as high as	highest the least high
tired	more tired not as tired as	the most tired the least tired
incredible	more incredible not as incredible as	the most incredible the least incredible

3. Prepositions of time: *until, after*

   Prepositions of place: *through, on, below, around*

   Prepositions of cause: *thanks to, because of*

CHECK OUT SENTENCES!

Statements and questions

I've never made a robot. ✓

When did Jamal make the robot? ✓

Has Jamal ever made a robot before?

Jamal brought his robot in to show in our science lesson.

Commands and exclamations

Ask an adult to help you put the biscuits in the oven. ✓

What a lot of mess you've made! ✓

What a good cook she is!

Offer Nanny a biscuit.

How helpful you are!

Subject and object in sentences

(Guinea pigs) *are rodents.* (Guinea pigs' teeth) *never stop growing.*

Our class snake, Bob, escaped from <u>his cage</u>.

Bob frightened <u>all the children in the reception class</u>.

He climbed to the top of <u>a very tall tree</u>.

(A spider) *ran up* <u>Miss Jensen's arm</u>.

(Zooey) *grabbed* <u>a glass</u>.

(Troy) *tried to catch* <u>the spider</u>.

Quick Quiz: Sentences

1. *Poppy, please shut the door.* **C**

   What an annoying laugh that woman has! **E**

   How long are you staying for? **Q**

   When will you come to my house? **Q**

   My teacher really liked the horror story I wrote. **S**

   Stop looking at your phone while at the table. **C**

2. (I) *want* <u>hot chocolate</u>.

   (My parents) *won't let* <u>me</u> *go to Alice's party.*

   How does (your phone) *take such great* <u>photos</u>?

   (Mr Townsend) *cancelled* <u>drama club</u> *today.*

3. Sample answers:

   Statement: *This donkey has big teeth.*

   Question: *Why is that donkey showing its teeth?*

   Exclamation: *What big teeth that donkey has!*

   Command: *Stop doing that.*

Noun phrases

a pair of brand new trainers ✓

I've got <u>a black and white sweatshirt</u>.

There's <u>an enormous sports shop</u> *in the centre of town.*

<u>Our grumpy PE teacher</u> *made us run around the playground.*

Adverbial phrases

I left my new trainers <u>at school</u>.

I get up early every morning <u>to go for a run</u>.

<u>After lunch</u>, *we went on the trampolines.*

<u>At the end of the walk</u>, *we had to go through a river.*

<u>In the middle of the forest</u>, *there was a trail back to the cabins.*

Clauses

<u>My favourite fruit</u> (is) *kiwi fruit.*

after <u>I</u> (ate) *all the fruit,*

<u>Apples</u> (grow) *in Britain.*

when <u>my mum</u> (gave) *me a banana,*

<u>The lovely red strawberries</u> (tasted) *delicious.*

Jai never eats apples. ✓

because he's allergic to apples ✓

Quick Quiz: Phrases and clauses

1. <u>Last year</u>, *my football team won the cup.* **A**

   The ball hit me <u>from above</u>. **A**

   It was a <u>wet and rainy day</u>. **N**

   I was covered in mud <u>by the end of the game</u>. **A**

   <u>After the match</u>, *I went to the cinema.* **A**

2. *Just before bed, I read a chapter of my book.* ✓

   Last night, I had a crazy dream. ✓

   Trying not to laugh, George looked down at his book. ✓

3. Noun phrase: a, Adverbial phrase: c, e, Clause: b, d

Compound sentences

I'm good at drawing, but I'm not so good at acting. ✓

My mum is learning French and she is learning Spanish. ✓

Sample answers:

I <u>go swimming</u> *and I* <u>play tennis</u>.

I don't <u>like computer games</u> *but I do* <u>like board games</u>.

Co-ordinating conjunctions

I don't know anything about where dinosaurs lived <u>or</u> *what they ate.*

I'm really interested in dinosaurs <u>and</u> I have a lot of books about them.

I used to be frightened of the skeletons in the dinosaur museum, <u>but</u> I'm not any more.

Quick Quiz: Clauses and co-ordinating conjunctions

1. I've got two brothers (but) I haven't got a sister.

   We went on a school trip to London (and) we went to Buckingham Palace.

   I fancy fish fingers for tea (but) I think we're having pasta.

2. *My dad likes basketball but he doesn't like football.*

   I don't know what I would like for my birthday or where to have my party.

   We could go to the park or we could go to the zoo.

Complex sentences

Hazel was riding her bike <u>when she saw the squirrel</u>.

Dad was cooking pancakes <u>because it was Pancake Day</u>.

<u>Although it was only 10 o'clock</u>, Maisie and Eva had a midnight feast.

Although she's very old, my nan still has all her own teeth.

Fred was angry with me because I ate his chocolate.

While Mum was shopping, Nathan cleaned his bedroom.

Subordinating conjunctions

<u>When</u> Henry VIII's brother Arthur died, Henry married his brother's wife.

Henry VIII beheaded his second wife <u>because</u> he wanted to marry someone else.

Henry changed his mind about wife number four <u>once</u> he had met her.

<u>If</u> Henry VIII was bored with his wife, he found a new one.

Henry VIII had a servant to carry his personal toilet everywhere with him <u>because</u> he was the king!

Relative clauses

That's the (cat) <u>which scratched me</u>.

That's the (park) <u>where I fell off the climbing frame</u>.

This the cake (that) I made yesterday.

She's the dinner lady (who) made me eat beetroot.

Can you remember the name of the restaurant (where) we had that lovely pasta?

The beans, <u>which were very hot</u>, tasted delicious.

Hannah, <u>who is my best friend</u>, loves macaroni cheese.

Mushrooms, <u>which are my favourite vegetable</u>, are a type of fungus.

Mack, <u>who goes to karate with me</u>, has just become a vegetarian.

Quick Quiz: Complex sentences, subordinating conjunctions and relative clauses

1. *George loves it when his little brother, <u>who is only three</u>, can't stop laughing.* ✓

2. *That's the person who runs football club.*

   Although I was very hungry, I waited to eat with my friends.

   In maths, which is my favourite lesson, we're doing angles.

3. *There's a supermarket on the field <u>where</u> I used to play.*

   In the shop I met a woman <u>who</u> lives on my street.

   I want a horse <u>although</u> I can't ride.

   That's Dan, <u>whose</u> daughter is in our class.

   <u>When</u> I leave school, I have to text my dad.

CHECK OUT TENSES!

The simple present

I <u>hunt</u> monsters as a job. Until last year, I worked in a fish and chip shop with my sister, but it bored me. My sister <u>hates</u> her job – she <u>peels</u> potatoes all day.

There *are* monsters all over the world. Nowadays, you *see* them everywhere. My sister *finds* them asleep in her garage all the time. They *pop* up in some strange places!

The present progressive

Simple present	Present progressive			
		Verb *be*	Second verb plus *-ing*	
I read.	I	am	reading	a book.
You ride your bike.	You	are	riding	your bike.
He/She/It feels sick.	He/She/It	is	feeling	sick.
We walk to school.	We	are	walking	to school.
They play football.	They	are	playing	football.

It is raining. ✓

The children are yawning. ✓

The present perfect

I know how the story ends because I <u>have watched</u> the film.

Example answer: I haven't got a pet.

Quick Quiz: Simple present, present progressive and present perfect

1. *I am writing a story about ghosts.* **PPR**

   I have read all the Harry Potter books. **PPF**

   Gemma and Emily are playing a game. **PPR**

   Priya likes bananas and sugar on toast. **SP**

   My grandad has never played a computer game. **PPF**

2. *Ben _____ to school because he missed the bus. I hope he gets there on time.*

   is walking ✓

   What a mess you have made! You _____ all your raisins on the floor.

   have dropped ✓

The simple past

Sheila always (wanted) *to be a knight, but her parents* (said) *that only boys* (could) *be knights. This* (made) *Sheila angry, so she* (took) *her father's sword and* (left) *home. She* (walked) *for many miles and for many days, until at last she* (arrived) *at the castle of Queen Hanaka, where her dream* (came) *true.*

love (kicked) (changed) (moved) save watch (asked) (wanted) decide (shoved)
liked, discovered, shouted, laughed

The past progressive

Simple past	Past progressive			
		Was or were	Second verb + *-ing*	
I ate the toffee.	I	was	eating	the toffee.
You walked the dog.	You	were	walking	the dog.
He/She/It slept.	He/She/It	was	sleeping	
We waited for Mum.	We	were	waiting	for Mum.
They practised guitar.	They	were	practising	guitar.

The waves were crashing onto the beach. ✓

He was looking on the ground for something. ✓

The past perfect

When you arrived, I <u>had</u> already <u>left</u> for school.

We had waited for ages.

Quick Quiz: Simple past, past progressive and past perfect

Dad had tried to make a chocolate cake. **PPF**

Ryan hadn't bothered to do the washing up. **PPF**

Tara and Ayisha were wondering what to do. **PPR**

Selma brushed her hair. **SP**

The waiter brought our drinks. **SP**

2. *Dad made a cake for Mum, but the dog*

_____ it before she got home.

had eaten ✓

While Dad _____ a nap, Jayden decided to play a computer game.

was having ✓

Modal verbs

They <u>may</u> have gone to Saeed's house.

The film <u>can't</u> have started already.

I <u>have to</u> go to town later today. ✓

Quick Quiz: Modal verbs

1. The girl had forgotten her coat – she must have been cold. ✓

   I might be visiting my cousins at the weekend. ✓

   You may get into the swimming squad this year. ✓

   I had to help my mum wash the car. ✓

   We could have ice cream for pudding. ✓

2. I'm not sure where Kayla is. She <u>might</u> have gone to the shop.

   My singing teacher is going away, so choir practice <u>will</u> stop over half term.

   You <u>can</u> still join the team, as we need one more player.

3. He might have fallen off a ladder. ✓

CHECK OUT PUNCTUATION!

Capital letters and full stops

New stars are called protostars. ✓

(galileo) was from (italy.)

(he) was born in the town of (pisa) in 1564.

(galileo) made the first proper telescope.

(in)(january) 1610, he was the first person to see that (jupiter) has four moons.

(he) also observed the planets (venus,)(saturn) and (neptune.)

Question marks and exclamation marks

Is it time to go home? ✓

What a lovely time you've had! ✓

Quick Quiz: Capital letters, full stops, question marks and exclamation marks

1. Where is the party**?**

   It's in the church hall**.**

   What fun you'll have**!**

Don't forget to take the present.

2. Mrs Ainsley gave me a big chocolate egg for Easter last March. ✓

3. Answers will vary.

Commas

In my salad, I don't want any lettuce, olives, carrot, tuna, red pepper or cheese.

I love my parents, Superman and Wonderwoman.

No cycling, horses or dogs allowed in the park.

Most of the time, travellers need a passport.

Today, we're going to cut out and glue, kids.

At the weekend, we're going to a pizza restaurant.

Pizza, which is comes from Italy, is very popular in the UK.

Before Niall tasted it, he could smell that the fish was not fresh.

Brackets and dashes

Snails – which are a type of mollusc – are eaten in France and Spain.

I'm never going to eat snails – that would be disgusting.

In China (where pandas come from) people speak many different languages.

I've never used chopsticks (I don't own any).

My dad (who travels a lot for work) went to China last year.

In Beijing (which used to be called Peking) he saw the Chinese State Circus.

Inverted commas/speech marks

Jack said, 'Hurry up! The shop is closing.' ✓

'Mum wants to buy me some new shoes,' Saffir said.

Jack said, 'Can I get some new shoes too?'

Quick Quiz: Commas, brackets, dashes and inverted commas

1. I went to see Fred at the weekend – he's got a new kitten. **D**

   Fred's kitten (just ten weeks old and very cute) likes chasing a ball of wool. **B**

   While I was playing with the kitten, Fred fed his hamster. **C**

2. For supper, we had hot chocolate, cheese on toast and sticky toffee pudding. ✓

3. Danni said, 'I really enjoyed swimming today.'

Colons

Jade has got three pets: a horse, a cat and a dog.

Children can choose from the following activities:

- *rafting*
- *gymnastics*
- *climbing*

I haven't got any pets: my brother's allergic to animals.

Semi-colons

John opened the drawer; it was empty.

Sally's birthday is in November; John's is in September.

There are lots of things I have to do over half term: visit Grandma and Grandad; learn to play the guitar; build a castle out of plastic bricks; sell old toys at a car boot sale; and paint my bedroom walls orange.

Quick Quiz: Colons and semi-colons

1. *My legs are tired: I ran five kilometres.* ✓
2. *For my birthday, I got an enormous jungle building set; a remote-controlled car that can flip over; a new sweatshirt with stripes on it; and some great books on how to draw cartoons.* ✓

I can't come out to play: I'm very busy.

There are five people in my family: me, my mum, my dad, my sister and my brother.

At the farm, you can feed the lambs; help to milk the cows; brush the ponies; and collect the eggs.

Apostrophes 1

do not	*don't*
will not	*won't*
could have	*could've*
there is	*there's*
she is	*she's*
we will	*we'll*
we had	*we'd*
they would	*they'd*

<u>*I am*</u> *so upset. My cousin said* <u>*she would*</u> *take me shopping but now her* <u>*car has*</u> *broken down and she* <u>*cannot*</u> *come.* <u>*I will*</u> *have to stay at home!*

Apostrophes 2

This toy belongs to my dog. → *This is my dog's toy.*

The dancers' shoes. ✓

Quick Quiz: Apostrophes

1. *The policewoman* <u>*could not*</u> *understand how the burglar got away.* couldn't

   She <u>*did not*</u> *know that the burglar was still in the building!* didn't

2. *I am Leo's best friend.* **P**

   Leo's my best friend. **C**

   Gracie's best friend is Lin. **P**

3. *These are Poppy's puppies.*

CHECK OUT SPELLING AND VOCABULARY!

Plurals 1

spells

wizards

cats

owls

broomsticks

man – men

tooth – teeth

person – people

mouse – mice

foot – feet

Plurals 2

babies, eyelashes, dresses, boxes, witches, gases

mangoes, halves, thieves, heroes

Quick Quiz: Plurals

1. *geese* ✓

   swans ✓

   pizzas ✓

2. Sample answers:

   two wolves

   five strawberries

   three superheroes

   five kisses or crosses

Prefixes 1

undo, disappear, incorrect, misbehave

supermarket, redraw, unexpected, submarine, underage

Prefixes 2

mis → *wrong or bad*

in → *not*

re → *do again*

non → *without or not*

sub → *below or under*

pre → *before*

Nouns	Verbs	Adjectives
subway	*resend*	*invisible*
preview	*misunderstood*	
nonfiction		

Quick Quiz: Prefixes

1. *My little brother was in a lot of trouble today. My mum's phone magically <u>disappeared</u> this morning. Mum said that she was very <u>disappointed</u> in my brother. This made him very <u>unhappy</u>. He said it was <u>impossible</u> that he had taken it, as he had been in his bedroom all morning. Mum said that was <u>nonsense</u>. Anyway, the phone magically <u>reappeared</u> after lunch.*

2. Answers will vary.

Suffixes 1

frighten|ed   walk|ed   honest|ly   careful||ly   amaze|ment   cry|ing

Yana texts Joe every day. **SP**

Yana texted Joe at 11. **P**

Yana is texting Joe now. **PP**

Suffixes 2

scored, skating

happier, partying

chopped

humming

Suffixes 3

sickness

cheerfulness

builder

excitement

dancer

agreement

*Superman is a power**ful** superhero; however, kryptonite makes him power**less**.*

Suffixes 4

Mrs Moffitt called <u>loudly</u> to her sister, who was a little deaf.

You don't <u>usually</u> see owls in the day.

Henry had sewn his cushion <u>badly</u>, so all the fluff came out of the middle.

athletically, horribly, scarily, historically, nicely, angrily

Quick Quiz: Suffixes

1. *Umberto the parrot <u>danced</u> <u>comically</u> around the room. Grandad <u>laughed</u> <u>loudly</u> as Umberto swung on a trapeze. Then the parrot <u>cheekily</u> spat a seed at Grandad. Harriet was <u>looking</u> at Umberto in <u>admiration</u>. 'He's <u>amazing</u>,' she told Grandad. Umberto <u>nodded</u> in <u>agreement</u>. A wave of <u>tiredness</u> <u>suddenly</u> came over the little parrot and he <u>climbed</u> <u>carefully</u> onto Harriet's lap and fell asleep <u>instantly</u>.*

2. Answers will vary.

Word families

<u>action</u>, <u>act</u>or, re<u>act</u>, <u>act</u>ivity

kilo (means 1000)	graph (means write or record)	aud (means hear)
kilogram	*photograph*	*audience*
kilometre	*graphics*	*audition*
kilobyte	*paragraph*	*audio*

Synonyms and antonyms

cold → *chilly*

brave → *fearless*

old → *elderly*

huge → *massive*

talk → *speak*

sea → *ocean*

hungry → *full*

freezing → *boiling*

tall → *short*

quickly → *slowly*

wild → *tame*

beautiful → *ugly*

Quick Quiz: Word families, synonyms and antonyms

1. *a hundred* ✓

   The night was <u>dark</u>, the <u>horseman</u> was feeling <u>worried</u>.

   He wasn't <u>certain</u> his horse knew the way <u>ahead</u>.

   The bananas had gone <u>mouldy</u> and the apples were <u>rotten</u>. S

   The rabbit ran <u>fast</u> but the tortoise ran <u>slowly</u>. A

Homophones

I read a <u>tale</u> once about a cow with a magic <u>tail</u>.

part of an animal → *tail*

story → *tale*

I <u>heard</u> a <u>herd</u> of cows mooing.

listened to → *heard*

group (of animals) → *herd*

It makes me <u>groan</u> every time an adult says how much I've <u>grown</u>.

The bubble man <u>blew</u> <u>blue</u> bubbles.

<u>I</u> looked in the mirror and noticed that my <u>eye</u> was red.

Silent letters and unstressed vowels

what   sign   comb   knife   wrist   listen

Silent g before n	Silent k before n	Silent h after w
gnaw	knee	when
design	know	what
	knife	
Silent w before r	**Silent w before h**	**Silent b after m**
wrong	whole	dumb
wrist		thumb
		comb
Silent h before o	**Silent u after g**	**Silent l**
hour	guess	half term
ghost	disguise	calm
	guest	

list(e)n   und(o)ne   famili(a)r   happ(i)ly

Quick Quiz: Homophones, silent letters and unstressed vowels

I had to go to the nurse to get my <u>weight</u> checked.

They couldn't see the boat because of the <u>mist</u> coming off the sea.

You should never <u>waste</u> food.

I think I've had <u>too</u> much pudding.

<u>Would</u> you like to come to my party?

forgotten U

guard S

sign S

lamb S

honest S

different U

GLOSSARY

abstract noun a noun that refers to feelings, concepts or states that do not exist physically (e.g. hope, love)

adjective a word used to describe something or somebody (e.g. red, interesting)

adverb a word that gives information about a verb, adjective or another adverb, sometimes formed by adding 'ly' to an adjective (e.g. slowly, anxiously)

adverbial (phrase) a phrase that functions like an adverb

antonym a word that has the opposite meaning of another word in the same language

apostrophe (') a punctuation mark that is used to show possession or in contractions

article one of the words 'a', 'an' or 'the'

brackets () a pair of punctuation marks used either side of extra information in a sentence

bullet point (●) a small, round mark used at the beginning of each item on a list in which every item starts a new line

capital letter the form of a letter that is written A, B, C, etc, used for example at the beginning of a sentence

clause a special phrase that includes a subject and a verb; a clause can be a complete sentence

collective noun a noun that is used to refer to a group of things (e.g. family, team)

colon (:) a punctuation mark that is used for example in front of a list or a part of a sentence that explains something

comma (,) a punctuation mark that is used for example to divide clauses or items in a list

command a sentence or phrase that tells someone to do something

comparative adjective an adjective that is used to compare things (e.g. longer, darker, more beautiful)

complex sentence a sentence usually made up of a main clause and one or more subordinate clauses

compound noun a noun made up of two shorter words (e.g. windmill, hairspray)

compound sentence a sentence made up of two independent clauses (or simple sentences) joined by a co-ordinating conjunction

conjunction a word that links two words or phrases together; there are two types: co-ordinating conjunctions and subordinating conjunctions

consonant a letter of the alphabet that is not a vowel

contraction (*or* contracted form) a word that is made by joining two words but omitting a letter or letters (e.g. don't, I'm)

co-ordinating conjunction a conjunction that links two words or phrases together as an equal pair

dash (–) a punctuation mark used for example to add extra information in a sentence or to indicate a pause before part of a sentence

determiner a word that specifies a noun as known or unknown (e.g. the, a, this, my, some)

exclamation a sentence or phrase that begins with 'how' or 'what' and ends with an exclamation mark, used to express strong feelings such as surprise or shock

exclamation mark (!) a punctuation mark that is used at the end of an exclamation

fronted adverbial a word or phrase that acts as an adverb that goes at the beginning of a sentence (e.g. In the end, On the other hand,)

full stop (.) a punctuation mark that is used at the end of a statement

helping verb a verb such as 'be', 'have' or 'can' that goes with another verb to form different tenses or give different meanings

homophones words that sound the same, but have different spellings and meanings (e.g. bear/bare)

imperative verb a 'bossy' verb that tells you what to do (e.g. wash the car, tidy your bedroom, brush your teeth)

inverted comma one of a pair of marks (' ' or "") used in written language for showing what someone said (also called *speech marks*)

irregular irregular words do not follow the usual patterns of words of a similar type

main clause a part of a sentence with a subject and a verb. A sentence contains at least one main clause, which makes sense on its own

modal verb a verb such as 'can', 'could', 'may', 'shall', that is used with another verb to express, for example, probability, permission, ability, advice and obligation

noun a word that is used for a thing, person, place, substance, feeling, etc. (e.g. table, thought, energy, London)

noun phrase a phrase with a noun as its main part

object the person or thing that has the action of the verb done to them

parenthesis when extra information is added to a sentence using pairs of brackets, dashes or commas

past perfect the tense that is used to talk about things that happened before the main action started, formed with 'had' and a past tense verb, e.g. *They had already arrived.*

personal pronoun a pronoun that is used to refer to a person or thing (e.g. I, them, it)

phrase a group of words that are grammatically connected

past progressive the tense that is used to talk about things that were happening at a particular time in the past, formed with *was* or *were* and an -ing verb (e.g. *We were chatting.*)

plural a word that shows that you are talking about more than one person or thing (e.g. legs, churches, mice)

possessive adjective an adjective that comes before a noun and tells you that noun belongs to (e.g. my, his, your)

possessive pronoun a pronoun that shows who owns something (e.g. ours, mine, yours)

prefix a letter or a group of letters added to the beginning of a word or letters, which alters its meaning (e.g. **aero**plane, **il**legal)

preposition a word that tells the reader the relationship between things or people (e.g. near, by, under, towards)

present perfect the tense that shows past events and uses 'has' or 'have' and a past tense verb, e.g. *He has gone away.*

present progressive the tense we use to talk about things that are happening now, formed with a the verb *be* and an -ing verb (e.g. *I am making bread.*)

pronoun a word that is used instead of a noun (e.g. it, they, this, she, mine)

proper noun a name for things like people, places, historical events, organisations, days and months

punctuation marks used in writing that help it make sense to the reader (e.g. commas, question marks and full stops)

question a sentence or phrase that asks someone something

question mark (?) a punctuation mark that is used at the end of a question

relative clause a part of a sentence beginning with a relative pronoun, that gives extra information about a noun

relative pronoun a word used to link a clause to a noun or pronoun (e.g. which, that, who)

reported speech an account of what has been said, without using the exact words spoken

root word (*or* **root form**) the most basic form of a word

semi-colon (;) a type of punctuation that links two ideas, events or pieces of information

sentence a group of words that make complete sense on their own. A sentence can be a question, statement, command or exclamation. A sentence always has a subject and a verb.

simple sentence a sentence with one main clause, usually containing a subject, verb and object

simple present the present tense that is used for regular events and situations or states that do not change

simple past the past tense that is usually formed by adding 'd' or 'ed' to the verb

singular a word that shows you are talking about one person or thing (e.g. dog, tree, aeroplane)

speech marks inverted commas

statement a sentence that tells you something

subject the person or thing that does the action of a verb

subordinate clause a clause that depends on another clause in order to make sense

subordinating conjunction a conjunction that introduces a subordinate clause

suffix a letter or a group of letters added to the end of a word or letters, which alters its grammatical form (e.g. sweet**ness**, driv**er**)

superlative adjective an adjective that is used to show that something or someone has the most of a particular quality (e.g. best, cleverest, most ridiculous)

synonym a word that has the same meaning as another word in the same language

tense the way verbs are used to show the time (past, present, or future) that the writer is talking about

word family a group of words that all include a part that is the same or similar, so that the meanings are connected (e.g. happy, happiness, happily)

verb a word that is used to talk about an action or a state (e.g. walk, happen, understand)

vowel one of the letters a, e, i, o or u

word class a set of words that do or describe the same thing (e.g. verbs, nouns, adjectives, pronouns)